Shoelaces

Richard Easton

Shoelaces

JeffersonPoetry.co.uk

Printed by Biddles Books Ltd, Castle House
King's Lynn, Norfolk PE321SF

ISBN 978-1-915292-54-4

Shoelaces

Dedicated to my Dad

Jefferson Edward Easton QPM

14/04/1938 - 20/01/2022

Heartbroken.

Our family grieves
As your life comes to an end
Husband, Dad, Granddad
Friend

Foreword

I first wrote a poem in 1983 during the General Election campaign. It was about the nuclear arms race that was quite a thing at the time, with America and the Western Allies embroiled in a Cold War with the USSR.

It seems ironic that as I write this, Russian troops are invading Ukraine and the Russian President has his nuclear weapons on alert.

A 16-year-old version of me considered the investment in such weapons as futile, but also recognised the impossibility of ever ridding our world of such destructive devices.

I got something from writing that poem, but for whatever reason, didn't write another until around 2015, when, prompted by a Facebook post featuring some images of the School Magazine that my poem had been published in, I decided to write a poem for my wife, Michelle, to mark our 25th Wedding Anniversary.

I then went on to write several others for family members before looking for more diverse subjects.

Inevitably, I turned to my 30-year police career which has gifted me with so much to write about. Having written and selected the poems for this book, I can't help but notice the frequency with which death has featured over the course of my career. A policeman's lot...

I also found myself increasingly drawn to writing about nature and the trials that our wildlife endures, literally daily as the animals and the environment struggle under the pressure that mankind subjects them to.

I wanted to publish my poems, mainly so that my Mum could access them.

I self-published **'Words, Thoughts, Observations'** in Autumn 2020 and **'Rambling Through Lockdown'** in Autumn 2021.

Both were limited to 100 copies and raised over £1100 that was shared between several charities.

'Shoelaces' is comprised of my favourite poems taken from these two books as well as 30 new poems to compliment and hopefully add value to this showcase of my work.

Thank you, as ever to my poetry Sensei, Steven P. Taylor for all his support, inspiration, encouragement and generosity; to my school friend and EnjoyRadio.co.uk show host Lesley Atherton for providing opportunities and objectives that pushed and developed my writing, confidence and presentations beyond anything that I ever imagined.

Thank you to my Son, James Easton for designing the cover and to Debbie and Chris for the evocative photography perfectly capturing the image that I had in mind.

To everyone who supported and bought copies of the first 2 books, thank you. By doing so, you really boosted my confidence.

My thanks to you for buying this book, I hope I manage to convey the emotion that inspired each poem.

Finally, thanks to Michelle and Mum & Dad for all the love, support and encouragement they have given me.

I will love you forever.

R.

Contents

When I Joined

I joined 'The Job', in April 89
I reflect, and look back, such a bygone time
Trained for 14 sunny weeks at Bruche
a defining time, there ended my youth

Rent Allowance, Dental costs and Prescriptions
benefits we lost despite protestations
We earned £10,500 a year
Some Nicks had a bar where you could get a late beer

Each Division had a canteen
where you could get your Refs
To protect ourselves, we had wooden 'staffs'
We didn't have body armour, CS or Tazers
we had woollen trousers, and tunics, like blazers

The ashtrays in CID were stolen from pubs
We had an LIO, which is now called a HUB
The intelligence system was in Lever Arch Files
and a card index system that must have stretched miles

All statements and files were handwritten by you
checked by the Sergeant, you hoped it'd get through
mistakes were highlighted, by a thick red line
not bullying... development, you got it right next time

No grievance procedure, you just did as you were told
We went out walking, in the rain and the cold
We went out 'as a Relief' on Thursday before nights
for a beer and a laugh, and to put the wrongs, right

We'd walk, with our legs, around our beat
we had brew stops, we'd visit, to rest our feet
Probationers went out, and got wet, in the rain
4 quick changeovers a month really scrambled your brain

You always knew that your scrote was a thief
if he kicked off on arrest and demanded a 'Brief'
We gave evidence in trials, every month at Crown Court
each division had its own back-office support

And every Division has its own Chief Super'
Fingerprints were taken, with ink, on paper
No High Vis jackets or mobile phones
No Air Support, helicopters or drones

Every Division had its own shift pattern
and don't even think of going out with no hat on
Your application for Leave, may well get refused
The division had five computers that we couldn't use

Every Relief... was self-sufficient
our own Traffic, Dogs and Custody contingent
With dedicated Comms' staff
who once worked the same streets
and knew the Division, and the people you'd meet

The Bosses wore white
the 'Bobbies', blue shirts
the ladies were 'Policewomen'
issued with handbags and skirts

The girls got a 'sexist' allowance for Stockings
we had D Reg Mini Metros,
and you may find this shocking
but Panda Cars didn't have "blues" or "twos"
we pressed our trousers and bulled our shoes

If you locked up, you'd stay on, to complete the task
a request to come in late?   You dare not ask
But your overtime was paid, no 'half hour for the Queen'
if the 'Bail Bunny' said no, then your prisoner 'stayed in'

So, if you finished at 3, you'd be back on at 7
you could get your head down
when you had Refs at eleven
Standards were important, there's no denying
whenever you finished, your shirt needed ironing

A crime with no prisoner, came back every time
the DCI's Question... 'Where's the evidence of crime?'
A window smashed, a burglar around?
Minor Damage report, value £24

RTCs were RTAs
Giros were reported stolen on Thursdays
On every shift, we had plenty of Cops
no need for cardboard cut-outs in the shops

Every locker had been forced at some time
People got arrested for committing a crime
no 'Necessity for Arrest'
Just "You're nicked, mate"
Interviews were handwritten on 808s

You weren't a 'Student Officer'
you were 'in your Probation'
We had cops parading on at every station
Your Sergeant or Inspector would 'show you a visit'
A secondment secured to the Plain Clothes Unit

A prosecution file, might just be a 330
to check Insurance or Licence, we'd issue a HORTi
a Summons Green Card, Fail to Produce at the scene
Blow in the bag until the crystals turn green

A community centre that was once Cheetham Nick
Grey Mare Lane became a film set, Plant Hill, derelict
Collyhurst was demolished, Chester House too
Memories of a time when I worked with you.

Since this poem was written, Grey Mare Lane has also been
demolished. The demolition of Bootle Street, my Dad's first and final
station is imminent.
The end of an era.

Rachel Street

As new probationers arrive on Division
an itinerary by way of an introduction
to the job and the area, where we'll work

There is no doubt, that Death stalks these streets
it's best we're prepared, else whilst on our Beats
we might see something, nasty, and shirk

I'd never seen a dead body before
the morning that I walked through the door
of the Rachel Street Mortuary
I have a strong natural aversion
but sensed voyeuristic fascination
with the things I was destined to see

I was relieved, to hear
the post-mortems were done
The Attendant suggested
that we'd 'Missed all the fun'
as I wondered, to myself...

who the fuck applies for a job as a Mortuary Attendant?
A perfect role
if you like to work alone
with quiet people and disinfectant

But in the fridge
he had three he'd 'made earlier'
Actual dead bodies
that made my toes curlier

He proudly displayed them for us to see
an old man
an old lady
and a small baby

Processed, examined, and now at peace
Sewn up, chilled
and ready for release

Things that I now cannot 'un-see'
like the clinical efficiency
of the post-mortem room

A processing plant for a human cadaver
stark, functional and macabre
a place of darkness and doom.

Pressing the Button

I'm dressed like a cop
but I don't know what to do
The new Sprog on the Block
I haven't got a clue
Today's first objective
has been set for me
to check out a vehicle on the PNC
over the radio
the whole division can hear
mind and mouth
stricken by fear
my Tutor, Stella,
suggests I rehearse
the prospect leaves me
stuttering with nerves
the button I must press
feels like a detonator
the increasing stress
as I wait for the Radio Operator

"6198, to the PNC"
"Err, 6918, confirm your identity"
"3757 to Comms, 6198 is working with me"
"Roger 3757, thanks for that...
Go ahead, 69, err 6198, a vehicle or body?"
The entire Division are now listening
Hesitation,
as I rehearse my lines
my mouth has gone dry
but Stella says I'll be fine

The Phonetic Alphabetic
must not be forgotten
the Division tunes in
as I press on the button...

*"A vehicle please
On Cheetham Hill Road"*

So far so good
my message flowed

"Go ahead with the details..."

Increasingly confident

*"Alpha
267
Juliet...
Norman Elephant"*

BOOM!

The Custody Sergeant

A young PC's first solo arrest
under pressure, I've got to pass this test
the Custody Sergeant, a Supreme Being

A person who seems to know everything
totally on it, constantly assessing
a deity of the Cops it seems

I cringe when *He's* on, it adds to my ordeal
when I lock up late and stay on to deal
He seems so unhelpful and rude

I've been on 15 hours, I'm starting to stink,
I'm in need of a shower and gagging for a drink
and it's been ages since I had any food

This growling Sergeant who never smiles
and always wants to check my files
I feel that I need to impress Him

But He never gives credit, or so it seems
He runs Custody with a tight regime
He's really grumpy and intimidating

I cross every I, and dot every T
my nerves have got the better of me
I start again, I've got to get it right

I check the detail, every page, completely
but He still finds errors that I didn't see
and now it's approaching midnight

The offence investigated, proved and admitted
the file eventually, signed and submitted
the prisoner charged, bedded down and remanded

I'm back on at seven, in 6 hours' time
hungry, and filthy with Custody grime
I need a lift to my Nick, and I'm stranded

Twelve years later and that Sergeant is me
grumpy and stressed running Custody
I've upset a young cop doing her best

My excuse, I'm under pressure with 34 cells
there are doors being banged and nasty smells
I could have helped her, but now she's distressed.

The Jumper

On a November morning
a body is found
at the foot of the flats
face down on the ground
a lad in his twenties
who's been there for hours
before we got a call
from a girl in this tower
She'd heard a noise
but it was dark at the time
so she'd looked out again
at twenty to nine
and then she saw him
lying below
and looked up and noticed
an open window
on the 14th floor
the room locked from inside
we'll never know
the turmoil in his life
that caused such sorrow
or how sad at that time
who did he think about?
as he tried to decide?
how long did he sit there?
what swayed his mind?
once he'd climbed out...
that peace he would find
as he fell, was he sure?
that this was what he wanted?
a sorrowful scene
and his family haunted.

Dirty Protest

A custody cell
you are serving your time
in lawful 'Container' confinement
You are confrontation epitomised
the walls smeared
with your excrement

TAG with shields
an 'Angry Man' entry
you're restrained and put to the floor
You've smashed and eaten
the safety glass
from the light above the door

Given a shower
then new clothes to wear
then off to Hospital for examination
Your cell is cleaned
whist the X-Rays show
the wired glass that's in your 'system'

Then back to the Station
"It'll pass in due course"
that wire entangled glass
But I'm glad it's not me
who's got something like that
waiting to come out of my ass.

Heart Shaped Scar

On patrol, but off my beat
a car is parked, on a dodgy street
little signs I notice, to me it is clear
this car is stolen, and it shouldn't be here

I pull alongside, in my liveried van
and get out, wearing uniform, a policeman
as I notice the vehicle is insecure
I hear a noise, a closing door

But when the door was opened, a dog was pushed out
a bull terrier, with lots of teeth in his snout
intended to intimidate, but I wasn't moved
I noticed the chassis number had been removed

A back up call, as the threat is sensed...

and then it began.

My life about to change
as the door reopened, he charged into range
I thought he was joking
couldn't make out what he said
then shock as I realised, I'd been punched to the head

Again and again, disoriented, confused
I raised my guard, my head is bruised
I landed a punch, but as I start to fight back
the dog was set to, by an order to attack

Slow motion
as I assess this developing situation
His punches still land, but there's a new sensation
my body suffers elsewhere, as I'm punched again
there's a dog on my leg, and significant pain

A further assessment, whilst I'm still on my feet
Do I fight him, or the dog? Both, I can't defeat
I concentrate on the dog, as they continue to attack
I prise open his mouth, but the dog bounces back

I know I'm overwhelmed, as the teeth lock again
a crushing and tearing kind of pain
the punches don't hurt
but I sense trauma from my thigh
BANG! another fist lands as I'm hit in the eye

I retreat, cover my head and go to the ground
The dog's on my leg, as I'm dragged around
whilst a mother and child, walk to school unperturbed
a normal Thursday morning in this neighbourhood?

I curl up and protect as best as I can
an accomplice came out, and smashed up my van
As the sirens approach, he runs back in through the door
my battle is lost, I pass out on the floor

Then done... It was over, that was it
so much had happened in just one minute
from getting out of the van, to unconscious on the floor
the difficulties will be experienced
for 2 decades and more

A guy from the Direct Works helped me up to my feet
my uniform dishevelled, as my mates turn into the street
a warmth on my leg, drains down from my thigh
my face is swollen and there's a cut to my eye

To Hospital;
the nurses, recognised my distress
bruised, bloodied, and upset, I confess
clothing removed, the first time that I see
the wounds to my leg, did it eat part of me?

Injected, treated, cleaned, injuries dressed
upset, confused, pretty distressed
How did this happen? What should I have done?
If I'd been better prepared, I could have won

The hole in my leg, will form a heart-shaped scar
This dog bite's not stitched, the risk of infection is far...
too great, and if infected
it would need 'invasive treatment'
So the scar is left to form, as a tormentor, it's permanent

I hear on the radio, that the news has broken
'A Police Officer's in hospital...' my Mum will be shaken
I give her a call, before she discovers the truth
that I am the cop, talked about on the news

And then home
Sore, shocked, angry, confused
What? Why? Totally bemused
time off work, unable to walk
The long-term injury, I was unable to talk

Physical injuries healed after a while
The real blow delivered, after a 2-week trial
where a barrister conspired to his perjured defence
Causing further injury and significant offence

A barrister lead this farce in Crown Court
A regular defender of my assailant, who sought
to influence the Jury, who in turn failed to convict
Another assault, via an unjust verdict

Career and spirit, affected for years
desperate for help, but prevented by fears
that to ask for help, would betray further inadequacy
desperate that someone would notice, and help me

He served years 'inside' for other indiscretions
The Court's failure fuelled a crushing depression
The sense of injustice
I wanted to secure
a 'right' for the 'wrong', that happened in Court number 4

Whenever he was out, I sought opportunity
I stayed within the law, but I wanted him to pay
Then a chance 'in the shadows', taken and assured
a significant sentence, my justice secured.

Next of Kin

Details over the radio
your name and address
My job to pass a message
to deliver you distress

I compose myself
as I make my way
I practice the words
that I might say

It never gets any easier
though I've done it before
I take a moment to compose myself
and then I knock on your door

I see you approaching
through the frosted glass
your life about to change
with the message I'll pass

The shock on your face
soon changes to fear
seeing me in this place
you know why I'm here

You hope it's something else
as our worlds collide
but you know the truth
"Can I come inside?"

You offer me tea
you're trying to delay
not wanting to hear
what I have to say
"Would you like to sit down?
I have some bad news."
You wonder which loved one
you're about to lose

I say the words
Who, how, when and where
Your eyes drop to the floor
as you slump in the chair

I'm looking for a sign
that you'll be alright
and search for a friend
who can come here tonight

This irreversible change
that I've brought to your life
the sudden numbness
from normal to strife

The unfillable void
the sense of grief
I make you a tea
our acquaintance is brief

Then a knock at the door
that friend has come around
your time to grieve
the moment, profound

I take my leave
and close the door
In the car I reflect
we've not met before

But you'll never forget
when I came to your door...

The one time that we met
the day I imparted
news of a loved one
now sadly departed

"6198, a result when you're ready."
To Comms, over the air,
"The death message is passed,
the next of kin have been informed and are aware."

"6198, thanks for that,
I've got a domestic, it's just come in
a child has phoned via 999
Mum and Dad are fighting, again."

Domestic

I'm 23 years old
and I am here to advise
how you two
in your 40s
ought to live your lives
the difficulties you face
the medications you use
the stress of your circumstances
blowing your fuse
the drunken arguments
the impact on your children
your family in crisis
the conditions they live in

I've limited experience
at work and in life
but you're under arrest
for assaulting for your wife
a drunken domestic
my only constraint
that early next week
she'll retract
her complaint
and then next Sunday evening
we'll do it all again
this cycle of chaos
destruction and pain.

ACAB

All coppers are bastards
but who dragged you clear
from the car you'd been racing
whilst bladdered on beer?

All coppers are bastards
and other vile names
but who risked their life
as it burst into flames?

All coppers are bastards
but who rushed to your aid
when by anonymous phone call
death threats were made?

All coppers are bastards
but who saved your life
when you were stabbed in the leg
with a zombie knife?

All coppers are bastards
but who did you phone
When the 'big boys' you 'play with'
Were on their way to your home?

All coppers are bastards
but we weren't your foes
when a rival drug dealer
shot out your windows

All coppers are bastards
but when it all came on top
it was us that you turned to
you needed a cop

All coppers are bastards
until your past caught up
When the Karma you earned
got you all smashed up

All coppers are bastards
But who stopped the bleeding
when you got yourself shot?
For our help you were pleading

Some coppers didn't book off
At the end of their shift
An eternal duty
Their families bereft.

https://policememorial.org.uk/

Not Guilty

I'll nick your bike
I'll steal from your shop
I'll TWOC yer car
I'll manage a crop
I'll sell on the street
to the junkies I meet
but I'm innocent until proven guilty

I'll snatch her handbag
she's 80 years old
I'll burgle yer 'ouse
and tax yer gold
when it all comes on top
I'll assault a cop
but I'm innocent until proven guilty

I'll terrorise the estate
and intimidate
I'll look after a grow
that I cultivate
when I've sold all the weed
I'll launder the proceeds
but I'm innocent until proven guilty

I'll tax the poor
to make myself rich
I'll kill someone
and leave their body in a ditch
maybe I'll chance it
and do a Cash-in-Transit
but I'm innocent until proven guilty

I'll max out your cards
on Catalogue fraud
as your business struggles
I'll still extort
It's you lot I'm shaftin'
when I go out graftin'
but I'm innocent until proven guilty

And if I get arrested
I know my rights
a meal and a blanket
and to sleep through the night
a solicitor and a doctor
to make sure I'm alright
because I'm innocent until proven guilty

The victims are frightened
they won't give a statement
my solicitor advised me
just go 'No Comment'
when the Cops question me
to 'prove my intent'
because I have a right to remain silent

I'm described by my Barrister
'Of previous good character'
with a troubled childhood, you see
It's for the Jury to decide
beyond all reasonable doubt
and if not
then they MUST acquit me

"He has a job now Your Honour
and a child on the way
"he's cooperated with Probation
in every way
"his family are in Court
to support him today
"I recommend a community sentence"

I'll launch an appeal
if the Judge sends me down
the cost of the Trial
will be met by The Crown
my Brief will try get me
a suspended sentence
and see that Justice was done for society

This Society I pillage
that now funds my defence
and assures my rights
whatever the offence
I'll assault you
injure you
hate you
and kill you
and I'll walk when you find me "Not Guilty".

Poetic Justice

A drug dealer captured by the tricks
of undercover police tactics
Another, who once had flash cars
now just a wretched addict
The gangster who ambushed a cop
seriously injured as he fled
A bully who terrorised and murdered
has a gunshot to the head
A loveless union, a violent partner
who terrorised his wife
Lay on the bed, she'll suffer no more
he never saw the knife
Jailed: the child killer
angry because a baby cried
The armed robber who wreaked such violence
and by a violent end, he died
The sex offender who liked young children
now childlike in the prison
The burglar who fell and broke his legs
during the commission
The street robber, who attacked a Nanna
because he thought her frail
Now weak and vulnerable on The Wing
three years he'll spend in jail
The "TWOCer" killed when the car he'd stolen
was wrapped around a tree
The rapists attacking strangers
locked up with strangers in HMP
The pimp infected by the girl
he'd raped, exploited and sold
A gangster shot dead
who had killed a boy
who was only 5 years old.

The Unknown Officer

Another day at work
another routine incident
just like so many before

An abandoned vehicle
or a burglary
normality to restore

But different to any other
because today
I'm going to lose my life

As I arrive at the scene
the offender's still present
and he's in possession of a knife

High on the drug
that drives his offending
his thought processes, are distorted

Now I'm on the scene
this wasn't his plan
his crime has now been thwarted

Senses alert
as the incident develops
all options are assessed

He wants to escape
but my duty today
is to place him under arrest

A brief confrontation
then I fall to the ground
I feel my blood is spilled

An "Officer down"
a stab, not a punch
an erratic act, that killed

Tomorrow in The House
a stern-faced Prime Minister
will stand in The Commons and refer

To "a dedicated Officer
of the highest standing"
and the Opposition will concur

But until today
my colleagues and I
have been the focus of your disdain

"Institutionally racist"
"Corrupt" and "Lazy"
worn down by malicious campaigns

So keep your meaningless
self-serving words
that hold no value for those who you reference

And understand
that this once fine institution
has been destroyed by your hostile interference.

It's Alright for Some!

I went to a serious road accident
I'm still haunted by the scene
an old lady crushed by a flat back truck
after the traffic lights changed to green

I went to a concern for welfare
the windows were crawling with flies
It's a grim but regular occurrence
when a lonely person dies

I found a guy lying face down
the floor was wet and red
there were holes from where his blood was draining
from two gunshots to his head

I went to a prison suicide
you can imagine the welcome I received
a body cut down from the prison bars
my fault, his family perceived

I went to the death of an elderly gent
the central heating was on full blast
the condition of this poor chap
is an image that will never be lost

I went to a Jumper from a block of flats
his problems no longer important
the aftermath remains with me
the remains of this tower block resident

I went to a Home Office post-mortem
and watched as William was dissected
to establish, the cause of his premature death
the images, forever recorded

I went to a house fire, "Persons Reported"
the parents were frantic outside
their children were missing, as the inferno raged
and there was no way to get inside

A seven-year-old girl lying in bed
she looked as though she was asleep
her father identified her body to me
then I covered her up with a sheet

I once went to work on Monday morning
And didn't get home until late Thursday
This included an unbroken 40-hour shift
And they wanted us back in on Friday

I stopped to check a suspicious car
within 1 minute, I'd been beaten unconscious
both mental and physical injuries
from a thug with a dog, that was vicious

I retired after just over 30 years
my time, it seems, was done
"Retired? At your age? Bloody hell!
You lucky sod, I'll tell you what,
It's alright for some!"

Institutionalised

30 years of policing
a constable by rank
serving and protecting
with little if any thanks

30 years of duty
in service of The Crown
inappropriate dark humour
it stops you getting down

30 years of policy
and following procedure
acknowledging hierarchy
moulding this strange creature

Uniform, in both
appearance
and in mind
interpreting the mood
becoming 'One of a kind'

You always know how your mate will act
in any given situation
predictable responses from any Cop
anywhere across the Nation

Obedience to lawful orders
alert and always assessing
'Standby, Standby, Standby'
'Clear Left' and 'Yes Yes' yessing

A dedicated Service
that so many folk malign
the unique British Police Force
the ever thinner, Thin Blue Line

It is the best job in the world
and we hold it so close to our hearts
so I'll finish this poem
with a quote
from the Author, Michael Marks

'And maybe just remind the few,
if ill of us they speak,
that we are all that stands between
The monsters and the weak.'

Service

The prisoners revolted
an inmate assaulted
I was with you when you died

A device detonated
a city centre devastated
I was there as glass fell from the sky

An old lady is stuck
underneath a truck
her cries still haunt my mind

When you wanted to drown
I fought you down
your 'Stay Alive' note was kind

A gangster executed
his body, I located
the hands, silently... screamed

When you ended your days
K3-09 in Strangeways
your felony, it seems, redeemed

A prison suicide
hung at dawn
a noose crafted from torn prison sheets

The heroin dealers
exploiting the weak
we took them off the streets

As you took your last breath
I reported your death
ensuring that the evidence was true

As they opened your chest
for a Coronial inquest
I was there looking into you

At the Coroner's Court
I delivered my report
about an acquaintance that I'd never met

An arsenal recovered
the evidence secured
we neutralised the threat

People, kidnapped and tortured
as a gang war, erupted
the things that you did were evil

The whole gang captured
for years incarcerated
the repercussions, are still very real

When they kicked in your door
and raped you on the floor
we caught them and put them away

We chased their car
they didn't run far
their crimes proved by DNA

Whilst doing my job
I was attacked by a yob
bleeding, unconscious, defeated

Memories
of moments, of times now passed
that so many take for granted

And when I moved on
some new colleagues showed scorn
the scowls on their faces betrayed...

The contempt that they felt
for the job that I did
for 30 years, 3 months and 15 days.

On the 26th January
An event occurs each year
A thing you can set your calendar to
That might provide a little cheer

What is this thing, I hear you ask
Your excitement, I must stem
The darkness has started fading back
And it is still light at 5pm

These Troubled Times

We have a right to Freedom of Expression
the source, it seems, of so much aggression
fuelling a feeling of doom and depression
in these troubled times

Tolerance of opposing views
is not a term that you might use
if commenting upon the News
in these troubled times

To speak against the Media Line
to express a contrary opine
will see you isolated, that's the bottom-line
in these troubled times

Now political correctness it seems has woken
the reality and truth must not be spoken
else you'll be described as being outspoken
in these troubled times

I don't understand what you hope to achieve
dividing society, will bring no reprieve
and the outcome, I know, won't be positive
in these troubled times

Manipulative agendas, incited and poked
political ideology, cited and stoked
intolerance of others, nurtured, provoked
in these troubled times

Political theory, presented as fact
differing opinions violently attacked
the truth concealed, as society cracks
in these troubled times

The mood... that is there to sense
it seems is becoming more intense
it's so easy now to cause offence
in these troubled times

Your right to free speech, I will always defend
the insult I feel, I will pretend
had no effect, else I lose a friend
in these troubled times

But with the right to speak your mind
comes a responsibility to be kind
democracy is weak, I think you may find
in these troubled times

A Manchester Street Cop whilst at my peak
with insight and knowledge, now reluctant to speak
a social situation, the outlook is bleak
in these troubled times

I don't sit on the Left, nor on the Right
no political loyalty can I cite
but I feel increasingly stressed and uptight
in these troubled times

So this poem I've written may not convey
my thoughts or how I feel today
for fear of offending by what I may say
we are in troubled times.

Destiny

As metal penetrates flesh, again
Lives end, actually, and effectively, again
The dispute, won, so frivolous
One dead and seven convicted

of another inner-city homicide
Young men, who by postcode divide
So tragic it makes me shiver
An outcome that could have been avoided

A 'devoted father' aged 17
with a little guidance
what could he have been?
Values adopted that failed to deliver
now, just another statistic

Convicted of 'Joint Enterprise'
Such wasted opportunities
Terrible implications
A repeated characteristic

Millionaire Rap artists, set a path for you
Wannabe Rappers confirm it as truth
Unachievable goals and expectations
that you expect to come to fruition

You exist alongside a brutal culture
Under a system that hangs, above like a vulture
Ethics adopted from Gangster movies
A route to chaos and destruction

An assumed victim mentality
constantly negating reality
Your mantra: "Fuck da Police"
A voluntary social reject

Reliance on violence, guns and knives
More devastated, wasted lives
Another blackmailed business fails
that you claimed to 'protect'

A dreadful, heavy, gold linked chain
proceeds of your ill-gotten gains
Your life, so clearly, off the rails
as you demand 'Respect'

That chain around your neck is bondage
such a garish and ugly appendage
There's a subtle difference between respect and fear
that you fail to detect

On your journey to these alleged heights
you affirm so many stereotypes
With each day your future becomes more clear
because it seems your days are numbered

With no real leadership capabilities
and your arrogance creating enemies
a young buck intent on climbing your ladder
your 'empire' is being plundered

Loyalties fail as your control declines
and on your position, he has designs
a younger version of you, but badder
he's been nurtured in your shadow

The gang fractured as new alliances form
sleepless nights whilst in your 'dorm'
you know these lads are forming a queue
this time, you'll have to lie low

History repeated and perpetuated
ranks promoted and relegated
Drive-By shots intended for you
you're forced to dive for cover

Willingly detached from society
devoid of social responsibility
society continues, oblivious
as two more lads face up to each other.

As the people called out
There was no doubt
That the people called out
Who were in, and not out
Were not actually
called Out
And those who were called up
Were not called Up
Nor did they sign Up
When they signed up
And they didn't sign In
When they signed in
Nor did those called out
Who were not called Out
Sign Out when they signed out.

Pray

Extreme intent
desperate and urgent
reflecting my intention

No options remain
no more to explain
as I focus my attention

A prayer to my maker
driven by love
a plea for divine intervention

PLEASE!
PLEASE!
Words uttered in panic
in response
to this hopeless situation

PLEASE HELP,
PLEASE... DO SOMETHING
A telepathic communication

Directed to God
images, imagined
my solo dedication

Hands, clasped tightly
focus my message
to a higher deity

As the knuckles whiten
a single word
that conveys the anxiety

PLEASE!

Eyes tightly shut
praying really hard
focussing my mind, body and soul

PLEASE HELP!
PLEASE... DO SOMETHING
to help United score a goal.

134 Years

The Beautiful Game
simplicity, at its best
tweaked and changed
causing Fan's unrest

The Football Association
and Premier League
a money machine
that's driven by greed

Your partners in crime
Sky and BT
keep adding the pounds
they think we don't see

Their TV Deals
exploiting the fans
and stealing the Game
from the working man

The extortionate charges
you impose on the Pubs
this money isn't seen
by the lower league clubs

It's to your shame
that you exploit such loyalty
and ruin the game
to maximise royalties

That a Premier League player
earns more in a season
than a small club is valued
a significant reason

That my Town team of Bury
were expelled from the League
despite all the love
they were strangled by greed.

Bury FC 1885 - 2019

Legend

Imagine being the player who scored
the winning goal at Wembley
to win the FA Cup for your team
and secure a place in history

Your status earned
and forever concerned
with the World's oldest
football competition

You have now become
the answer
to a tricky
Pub Quiz question

The purists will ensure
you keep your place
in the record books

Forever a Legend
for your club's fans
for the second that it took

To put a ball across the line
under the bar
and between the sticks

Just like Bob Stokes
for Southampton
as they beat United
in 76

The ascension of Roger Osborne
Arsenal rue the date
that Ipswich Town won the FA Cup
in 1978

In 1987
it was Gary Mabbutt's left knee
that put the ball into his own net
to win the cup for Coventry

In 88, Liverpool
took on The Crazy Gang
Beasant saved
Sanchez Scored
as Wimbledon fans sang

In 2008
Kanu scored
forcing Cardiff tears
a domestic honour
for Portsmouth
their first for seventy years

2013 Wigan v City
surely Wigan
couldn't win it
But then Ben Watson stepped forward
and scored his goal
in the 91st minute

You won the FA Cup
that sunny day in May
you scored the winning goal
that can never be taken away

And some might say
that your moment
was so much more thrilling

Because of your goal
your FA Cup triumph
is described as a 'Giant killing'.

This is my land
This is my mine
This land is mine
This mine is mine
I mine the land
As I mine the land
This land is mined
This is my land mine
This land is mined
If you don't mind

Imagine our Monica playing Harmonica
With Annette on castanets
And a girl called Joanna
Playing the piana
Whilst Imogen sings 'No Regrets'

N2409, Row 3, Seat 72

Tommy Doc
depriving the Kop
of 'The Treble' in 77

Big Ron
with Butch and Robbo
securing an FA Cup heaven

Robson and Stapleton
dismantling
Maradona's Barcelona

Mark Robins
saving Fergie
when it seemed his reign was over

Mark Hughes with a brace
a Euro Final
with Sealy and 'Sunbed' in net

In the Rotterdam rain
in 1991
a night I'll never forget

Pally and Bruce
declare a truce
with Schmeichel as we win the league

This Fergie team
built on Jaffa Cakes
never showed fatigue

Cantona's telepathic flicks
with Kanchelskis on the wing
Hansen's ill-informed quips
'With kids you won't win a thing'

The Class of 92 came through
as a double is secured
these kids are destined
to win it all
their legacies are assured

Nicky Butt and Ryan Giggs,
the Nevilles,
Beckham and Scholes
this team, well oiled
us fans were spoiled
so many 'Fergie Time' goals

99, it was Andy Cole
and his Premiership winning chip
Scholes and Teddy made it a Double
on another Wembley trip

A Sheringham equaliser
then unbelievably
"Solskjaer has won it."
a unique and glorious Treble secured
by two goals in the final minute

I've no idea
how many times
I have sat on you

North Stand
N2409
Row 3
Seat 72

The legends who came
to the Theatre of Dreams
intent that they would beat
This 'Manchester United' team
I saw them all from this seat

Davids
Gullit
Shearer
Bergkamp
Hansen
Keegan
And Souness

Dalgleish
Rush
Romario
Klinsman
Figo and
Matteus

Maldini
Baggio
Zinedine Zidane
Stoichkov
Carlos
Nadal

Both Ronaldos
and legendary Reds
like Norman Whiteside
Et al

Roy Keane
and Denis Irwin
Lou Macari
and van Nistelrooy

Wayne Rooney
for Everton
coming on
as a 16-year-old boy

I've been blessed
to see
such history written
since I was a lad
Even more so
to have witnessed it all
sat next to my Dad.

Shoelaces

When we all had younger faces
you'd wipe my mouth and nose
You used to tie my laces
and help me with my clothes

When we all had younger faces
you'd get me something to eat
When we got into the car
you'd strap me in the seat

I jumped off a swing, and broke my arm
when I was only little
but you finished work, regardless
and took me to Hospital

Now many decades have passed by
our roles it seems, have changed
I don't know how you feel about this
but you mustn't feel ashamed

As you shiver
from the cold
I help you with your coat
I guide your arms into the sleeves
as memories are evoked

Memories recalled from a time
when I was just a lad
We all had younger faces then
and I had a younger Mum and Dad

I get your food and make sure you eat
I take your list to the supermarket
You have a Blue Badge in your car
so it's easier for you to park it

As I wheel you around the Hospital
a sad thought comes to mind
despite all the things we did together
there was so much wasted time

As I kneel on the floor
in front of you
we both wear older faces
I help you putting on your shoes
and then I tie your laces.

x

Time

Interests, pleasures
already experienced
unknowingly...
for the final time,
An old friend, met
for a drink and a chat
A song sang
to the very last line

A favoured place, visited
a last dance, a parting kiss
handshakes as we get up to leave
unbeknown to us both
we will never meet again
a 'goodbye' that this time, deceives

There's no fiercer predator
stalking every living creature
and winning without fail
It's Time
It keeps ticking away
by the hour, every day
as we slowly live out our lives

Walks in The Lakes
pasta or steaks
meals with family or friends
The slow tricks of time
have been tricking my mind
now too late
as my time, expends

And when I am gone
I'll watch over you
I'll always be around
if I can
and when your time comes
I'll be there to reassure you
To guide you and hold your hand.

Heartbroken

As your life ends
your soul ascends
I can't speak, my throat is aching
It is so strange
our lives, now changed
and inside, my heart is breaking

I hold your hand
and my body screams
as I say my last goodbyes
You lie there, still
and then I notice
there are tears in your eyes

All your memories
are now lost
like... tears, in the rain
I can't believe
that you have gone
and we won't speak again

This feeling of loss
the void you leave
you were one of my three towers
It's difficult
for us to imagine
how different your upbringing
from ours

Your once bright light
now dims and fades
our family, changed forever
Dependencies
exposed by your absence
we will toast you whenever we're together

As you join our family's
ascended elders
those family members who are now gone
now gathered to greet you
their souls will guide you
in our hearts, you will always live on.

Jefferson Edward Easton QPM
14/04/1938 – 20/01/2022

JRE
21ˢᵗ January 2022

Time to Say Goodbye

The song that was playing on the radio
as you exhaled for the final time
The tears that formed in your eyes
and also formed in mine

You taught me to thrive, Dad
you helped me through
your standards I adopted
You taught me to drive
you helped me grow
in every way, supported

Together, we won the FA Cup, Dad
and we triumphed in Rotterdam
We won The Treble in Barcelona
you, me, Solskjaer and Sheringham

We won the Premier League 13 times
and 9 FA Cups too
We travelled to Wembley 25 times
and a third European Cup to boot

Together, we conquered mountains, Dad
and explored the Lakeland tarns
We ventured the most extreme terrain
but never came to harm

We took Helvellyn's Edge in our Stride
we blunted Blencathra's Sharp Edge
Up and down Rossett Ghyll on our way up Bowfell
with a sheep stranded on a ledge

Do you remember Glaramara and Allen Crags?
Pavey Ark was such a treat
Cambridge Crag, such special memories
where we battered our poor feet

Haystacks, Cat Bells, Helm Crag too
The Lion and The Lamb
A trip to The King's Head in Thirlspot
gave a clue to who I am

Great Gable achieved on our second attempt
we got drenched on our first
Kirk Fell the steepest of our ascents
to the Inn to quench our thirst

A memorial walk up Wetherlam
a Halifax Bomber crew remembered
50 years to the day since that plane had crashed
The RAF had already attended

We took on Fairfield Hospital, Dad
we knew our case was just
we proved our point, to protect our James
we beat the NHS Trust

Family holidays with the Grand kids
Benalmadena and Tenerife
Quality time we spent together
more treasured memories

Family meals in restaurants
and many more at home
This Easton family that you built
on foundations you made so strong

We did it Dad, we lived our lives
as a Father and a Son
A friend, a guide,
you adopted my bride
we're heartbroken now you're gone.

JRE
31ˢᵗ January 2022

January

As February dawns
our family mourns
your loss has rocked us all

The treasured memories
we hold so dear
our tears continue to fall

Our love so strong
it seems so wrong
emotions that can't be spoken

Your life complete
we grieve your loss
the family left heartbroken

Your time is done
we'll look after Mum
and move on day by day

And as we do
it breaks my heart
to leave you in January

JRE
1ˢᵗ February 2022

Christmas Card List

Friends and relatives
whose time has passed
those who have now gone
Discomfort
thinking whether to delete
your details
from my phone

Names on our Christmas Card list
but no more cards to send
to cross you off
seems callous
and disrespectful
to a friend

Realising that...
of our times together
there are no photographs
taken in more
carefree times
capturing the fun and laughs

So many opportunities
but no images can be found
to prove our friendship
or the times
we went out on the Town

So I'll leave you in
as a reminder
So that I think of you next year
and as I write
I'll cherish the memories
of time spent
with someone dear

This list
a reminder
of who to send cards to
Is changing all the time
into a record
of people I once knew
people who were friends of mine.

Grief

The guilt that I feel
is so very real
we should be enjoying Our Time
Our working lives over
this should be our adventure
instead I'm alone for all time

People have stopped talking
to me, when I'm walking
I guess they don't know what to say
But this adds to the sadness
leaving me in a bigger mess
and more lonely than I was yesterday

Since you've been gone
I've been lost on my own
your absence just won't go away
I've not been my best
I've lost all my zest
and there's nothing that anyone can say

Alone in the house
I talk to myself
alone, there's nowt else to do
Alone in the car
a new burning scar
alone, always talking to you

Guilt when I realise
that I have got dry eyes
for a moment, I wasn't thinking of you
Crying, Not crying
a meal for one
alone in a bed made for two

Everything we own
all the things in our home
every item reminds me of you
I remember when we bought it
and I know you didn't like it
now I treasure that memory too

The difficult firsts
Christenings or births
should I bother with a Christmas Tree?
Our Anniversary
the Grandchildren's birthdays
writing a Card, to them, just from me

As I dry yet another tear
at the end of another year
I don't know how to deal with this grief
If you could only come back
I'd be right back on track
but I know that can never be.

A Funeral in Lockdown

Your final gathering
with your friends and family
together
in their best and finery
in keeping
with funeral
tradition

Your nearest and dearest
their memories spoken
of your antics, before
your life was taken
by a Pre-Existing condition

So many years, so many friends
so many memories,
now it ends
in this inappropriately
small event

So many others
who should have been here
paying respects and sharing a beer
but today
just a family lament

With limited numbers
there was no wake
no hugs for loved ones
no firm handshake
just some words
then that was that

So after what feels like
an inadequate service
broadcast to the World
over an interface
we disperse
it's all a bit flat.

Alan Dooley
4th Feb 1932 – 11th March 2021

Memories

Some Memories seem like yesterday
Though fifty years have passed
Some seem like fiction and unreal
Some memories didn't last

Happy times and carefree days
Some moments... lost forever
Friends at the time
The things we did
Things I now can't remember

"Do you remember when..."
I laugh along to the tale that you share
And I quietly wonder to myself
If I was even there

And those things I do remember
Are now all skewed by time
How accurate are the memories?
In my ever-fading mind.

A Tree in a Wood

A positive thing
From such a terrible loss
Of a dearly loved Son

A memorial tree
In a place of remembrance
That will grow as time moves on

Brought together in the love
Of those who they left
Now sitting in the shade

A wood full of people
Stand together, forever
Planted in the glade.

For Kay and David,
in memory of Tom

A Table for One

A table for two, in the window
But tonight
there is only one diner
Her favoured accessories
a special dress
Elegant in formal attire

'A table for one, please'
'A glass, not a bottle'
No small talk or discussions
An empty chair
Where your lover once sat?
No shared thoughts or ambitions

Surrounded by couples
Their laughter
and tales
Seem to mock your solitary meal
Alone, with a book
And maybe some memories
I wonder how you feel

A glass of red wine
That you didn't finish
Your food,
pushed around the plate
You alight from your chair
Descend by the stairs
And leave, alone with your soul mate.

Josephine

Eighteen years old
I'm under your spell
I'm completely
lost
without you
I'll give you my all
I'll do anything for you
only you can get me through

My desire
it's impossible to function
as my needs intensify
This, one way love
is my addiction
it's never satisfied

I'm lost when you're gone
the sinking feeling
as the emptiness returns
I need you more
my emotions reeling
my body, aches and burns

And then you're back
you can do no wrong
there's nothing to explain
I welcome your presence
my spirit lifts
now I have you back again.

The Homeless Guy

The wreckage of my life
that sits on the floor
near the cash machine
or the Supermarket door
With a cardboard cup
and a cardboard 'chair'
begging to survive
does anyone care?

A passing stranger
avoids eye contact
"Spare any change please"
how will he react?
A few quid if I'm lucky
maybe ignored or abused
resigned and alone
depressed and confused

Another group of young lads
What will they say?
"I earn my money"
"You chose to live this way"
Subjected to another
verbal assault
*"Get a job you lazy bastard,
it's your own fault"*

These consequences
that I face everyday
my poor decisions
what can I say?

A past that resulted
in me having to beg
I have nowhere to live
and shrapnel in my leg

I must fight for this spot
if I am going to exist
but it's hard to retain
if I'm stoned or pissed

It's difficult
to quit
I've
got a habit
to feed
Any shame
I once felt
now replaced by need

'Issues'
with alcohol
cocaine
and heroin
real human parasites
intent on exploiting

I'm addicted to Spice
and addicted to Khet
everything
that I own
is here
and wet

The cost to my health
the impact on my life
it cost me my family
my home and my wife

So I live on the street
no friends I can trust
no future
no family
no purpose
I'm bust
No ambition or drive
the life I once had
cannot be recovered
I was once a Dad

Now living in a
perpetual moment
a Groundhog minute
I've done my atonement

But this is 'my lot'
imagine my plight
sleeping in a carpark
every night

My head aches from the chemicals
nulling memories
brought back
from 2 years in Afghanistan
and three tours of Iraq

The vulnerability
of my broken mind
alone and compromised
please try to be kind

Just say 'Good morning'
as you walk on by
I served my country
and saw my friends die.

Spare Any Change?

"Can you spare any change please?"
Vulnerability displayed
in the street
for all to see

"No problem, God bless, have a nice day"
As you all walk past me

"Any spare change, Mister?"
Maybe he didn't hear me
with that gorgeous girl
whispering in his ear

No way out of... this thing
nowhere to go
no longer any tears

"Spare any change, Miss?"
she's so confident
as she just walks on by

A businessman on his mobile phone
I try to catch his eye

"Any spare change Sir?"
the stress on his face
as he works to secure a deal

The short dated food
and leftovers
that will make up my next meal

"Can you spare any change please?"
for chemicals
the addiction that they feed

So many issues
that drive my decline
It'll help me to get what I need

"Can you spare any change please?"
it'll make it easier
when I'm rattlin'
to block out the pain

"Can you spare any change please?"
It will help me to cope
with another cold night in the rain

A young girl
living like this
on the streets
I don't recognise
The dangers you see

I just do what I must
To exist through today
"Any spare change?"
Really means,
"Please, Help me".

Borders

The imaginary lines
put in place to divide
and keep people over there
and not here
But the birds don't care
as they fly through the air
and return freely again
every year

Territorial boundaries
a village, or a city
a county, or a nation
But the clouds don't care
drifting freely through the air
carrying a deluge of irrigation

Butterflies dance
over a field, in France
amongst the poppies
where so many lives ended
But the flowers don't care
their pollen, carried in air
across the lines
those young men defended

A wall of division
that isolates Mexico
from Trump and his greed driven lies
To control a population
whilst ignoring the pollution
that blows freely across our skies

A 'presidential' vision
of a Russian invasion
with tanks crossing lines in the snow
Controlling resources
whilst ignoring the voices
as we wonder how far this will go

Those lines on a map
denoting the territory
and the National boundary
it confirms
But Covid19 didn't care
as it spread through the air
human boundaries
are irrelevant to germs.

I Saw You on the Tele

I watch your plight
on TV News
live, as events unfold
whilst relaxing in my living room
there's a story to be told

Stuck in a warzone
powerless
witness to this Russian invasion
terror and vulnerability imposed
by unjust Russian aggression

This situation that you're dealing with
your life
a world away from mine
terrible scenes, of war and horror
as I sit here drinking wine

Unaware of what's really happening
a child
plays in the snow
defenceless and oblivious
a child I'll never know

Vladimir Putin
like a mad Rasputin
indifferent to this destruction of lives
A family trying to get out
are killed in a shoot out
whilst this psychopath spins his lies

A pretty young girl
and her family shot dead
as they desperately tried to flee
Murdered, for nothing
they posed no threat
to the might of the Russian Army

Ukrainians, and
their desperate situation
the images stir and evoke
compassionate feelings
such strong emotion
whilst Ukraine is shrouded in smoke

As I relax in my home
in comfort and safety
as another busy day ends
normal people
just like you and me
risk their lives
for the Country they defend.

People Just Like Us

So many normal families
Families just like ours
Husbands and wives
And children
Victims of a Superpower

A grandmother's memories
Of a time
When this happened before
Her wisdom means she understands
That it's the people who suffer in war

The fathers
Fighting to repel
a stronger Russian foe
Will he ever see his family again?
He really doesn't know

As mothers
Leave their lovers
With their kids, as refugees
A woman's strength
As they flee the horrors
Brought by the Russian armies

The children
Tired and hungry
Not understanding what is happening
No play or school
A situation so cruel
As their nation takes a hammering

The pets
Left abandoned
When their owners had to flee
Now feral animals
Forage in rubble
Looking for something to eat

The friends
Separated
Not knowing if they'll meet again
They flee a war
Waged on their town
This war is inhumane

The communities
Devastated
The infrastructure destroyed
Mariupol
Now resembles Hiroshima
From the missiles Russia deployed...

against civilian targets
Normal people
People just like us
So many killed
Their bodies lie
In the rubble and the dust.

Disasters Emergency Committee
www.dec.org.uk

Acceptance

We're all a bit unique
We all have our differences
We can all be a little bit weird
With our own individual nuances

Some say, we're *all* autistic
that we're all somewhere on the Spectrum
we can all be a little bit awkward
in a difficult situation

But what makes a situation 'difficult'?
And why does it make me feel awkward?
We all have our individual preferences
And issues to be conquered

So try not to be ignorant
Accept people and acclaim
The fact that we are all different
Means, in a way, we are all the same.

Wee cud chews two tork
and waist Ann hour of ure thyme
ass aye no yew new,
ore
weighting fore a brake inn the reign
eye through a peace of would
write threw that whole their
braking your knows and a pain

A Crash on the Motorway

640am
A November morning
in driving rain
visibility appalling

On the M60, clockwise
I briefly see
a smashed up car
just 10 feet from me

But on the opposite side
and facing the wrong way
a small car,
stopped
in the outside lane

The front end smashed
the engine steaming
cars flying through
the rain is teeming

Terrifying vulnerability
just seconds to act
reduced visibility
you need to react
and get out of that car
into the Central reservation
the Hard Shoulder's
too far
as a safe destination

It's just a matter of time
before someone pulls out
into the outside lane
and wipes you out
in this terrible weather
I wonder who you are

I hope you're alright
and got out of the car
and made it to safety
hopefully unhurt
whilst I drove past you
on my way to work.

Roadkill

As if life wasn't already hard enough
as if they didn't already have it so tough
This evening at dusk, an amorous toad
didn't quite make it across the road

A hedgehog forages, clearing gardens of slugs
then crosses a road in search of more bugs
As a car speeds through a residential estate
another casualty left in a terrible state

As if life wasn't hard enough, anyway
a Vixen lies injured, on the Motorway
her cubs in the Den, waiting for a meal
they won't eat the hen that she'd managed to steal

Birds, like pheasants, who swoop when they fly
it seems that they have, evolved, to die
as they fail to judge their flightpath to precision
a lorry approaches, an inevitable collision

As if life wasn't so cruel everyday
for a badger there's now a dual carriageway
a central reservation and two extra lanes
he'll never return to the Sett again

Instinctively timid, all species of deer
they often bolt without thinking, in response to fear
as they charge over a hedge into once familiar terrain
where there used to be saftey, there is now a train

So many creatures, every year fall victim
domestic pets, magpies and pigeons
buzzards, rodents, a rabbit or squirrel
they're easier to dismiss
if you just call them roadkill.

The Angels of the North

They dug the canals
they built the Mills
they dug the tunnels through Lancashire hills

With picks and shovels
to build and construct
the aqueducts and the viaducts

Enriching the nation
generating wealth
an industrial revolution
at what cost to their health?

As they farmed the fields
and dug the coal
a life underground that took its toll

The Ship Canal
connected the North
to the four corners of the Earth

And attracted a workforce
united by hope
that couldn't be any more diverse

Their homes were squalid
their appearance, pallid
through disease and malnutrition

The dreadful homes
where they simply existed
in diabolical deprivation

So as the nation prospered
through the toil
of the Angels of the North

The cotton towns
began to sprawl
recruitment grounds for the wars

These 'Worker Bees'
who gave their all
were worked into their graves

They died by the thousand
no reward for their labour
these people were surely slaves.

Two Minutes of Your Time

Sixteen million killed, in World War One
sixty million in 'The Second'
often just lads, with a dream of adventure
where Service and National Pride beckoned

When they were 'called'
they marched off to battle
these Pals from Lancashire

To fight the wars
and defend the Realm
against hostile gunfire

The 'misrepresentation' of their prospects
masked what they were destined to endure
the hidden truth of what lay ahead
such unimaginable horror

Since the 'War to end all wars'
we've had many new 'Campaigns'
each the source of a family's grief
a young soldier's repatriated remains

A cross now stands
bearing the names
of so many deceased young men

A small white Gravestone
where they now rest
they never saw their village again

Lifetimes lived, so much time has now passed
those of us who now reside
in this green and pleasant land
never knew those Men who died

So, the least that we, 'The Many' can do
is to stop... and pause to remember
the sacrifices, of 'The Few'
on the 11th day of November.

Imagine... What if?

What if things weren't as they are?
Imagine life without a car
What if you had no mobile phone?
What if you didn't have a home?
I mean, really... what if you were homeless?
Where would you put your stuff?
What if you lost your job?
Imagine living rough
No bedroom, No bathroom, No kitchen...
No high-speed wireless connection...
or Freeview, no tele... Imagine it...
What if there was no internet?
What if you had no fridge freezer?
How would you keep your meat?
What if you had no bread?
What if you had nothing to eat?
How would you feed the birds...?

How would you hang up the washing...
if you had no pegs?
What if you didn't have a washing machine?
What if you had no legs?
Imagine needing a wheelchair...
How different your life would be
What if you lost your hearing?
What if you couldn't see?
Imagine if you went deaf
Imagine being blind
What if you didn't understand... anything?
What if you lost your mind?

What if you didn't recognise yourself?
Your kids? Your family?
What if your life was desperate?
What if you had no money?
What if you lived on skid row?
What if you had no friends?
What if you had nowhere to go?
No Christmas cards to send
What if you were lonely?
What if nobody cared?
What if you had no family?
Imagine...

When The Fun Stops...

I feel a thrill as I open the App
and check the form and handicaps
I check out the Odds and choose a nag
I've got this one, it's in the bag

I set my Stake, a Single 'To Win'
my weekly wages, I go 'All In'
this one's a dead cert', my money 'invested'
I'll get every penny back, the winner selected

I'm on a roll, as my horse romps home
the winnings drop in, at 30 to 1
this is 'The One', I'll be adored
when I take them all on a holiday abroad

I put half my winnings on an accumulator
four bets to win, the winnings roll over
I've done this before, it's just a flutter
what She doesn't know, can never hurt her

The first horse falls, and with it, the bet
that shouldn't have happened, my hands start to sweat
I've lost half my money, but I'm still up on the day
but now it's only a Blackpool Holiday

Dreaming of that beach in Spain
I open up the App again
chasing my losses, A Double, A Yankee
I get better Odds if I back a 'Donkey'

One final bet as I'm on the chase
one of these horses will win this race
I back the favourite, to win 'Each Way'
I've got to go home with some money today

I'll stop off at the Food Bank
to get us some tea
I'd have won thirty grand
if they'd come in for me
I was unlucky today
every race has it's Winner
Thank God that the kids get a free School Dinner

I've never even been in a Betting Shop
the adverts say "When the fun stops, STOP"
but it wasn't much fun and there's no holiday for us
I lost all our money, travelling home, on the bus.

Man's Best Friend

A relationship repeated a million times over
one man and his dog, his master's voice
sheep dog
police dog
guide dogs for the blind
more than a pet, loyalty defined

Your every move monitored, with anticipation
that the reason you got up
might bring some attention
a stroke
a snack
or maybe small talk
or if I'm really lucky
we might go for a walk

A knock at the door
a chance to pretend
that I am ready and strong
and able to defend,
against
the postman
the paperboy
the window cleaner
all threats
in my mind
I'll see off the 'offender'

A ball or a rope
anything you want to do
I'm happy to do anything
if I'm with you
stay in
go out
do nothing
that's fine
we'll stay here at home
we can both have a whine

Then... I am taken...
by a less loving man
who came by one day
and put me in a van
Other dogs
no food
and nothing to do
no sign of my owner
does he miss me too?

I'm stuck in a cage
next to another hound
there's a treadmill
and a tyre to drag around
no love
no play
it's all very stressed
some dogs disappear
some come back a mess

I'm taken to a building
there are lots of men
some other dogs
but I don't know them
Thrown in
shouting
I'm bitten and injured
I have to fight back
I'm bleeding and cornered

The cheers and jeers
of the men that surround
the pit we are in
it's a frightening sound
fighting
biting
I'm under attack
unsure what to do
I need to fight back

Suddenly
I've been got by the throat
the other dog has me
I'm in trouble
I know
breathing... bleeding...
the pain seems unreal
shouting, noises...
quieting
it's strange how I feel

I was no match
the other dog won
I'm lying
dying
the men had their fun
injured
killed
no need for a vet
for the price of my life
some men won a bet.

The Bull

The Running of the Bulls, 'La Corrida de Toros'
an event devoid of culture or kudos
He really hasn't got any chance
His capabilities negated in advance

He is taunted for your cruel satisfaction
panicked hooves on cobbles, that provide no traction
His horns are blunted, to remove his threat
you add to his torment, fireworks are set

The first encounter, he doesn't understand
developed expertise, deployed to confuse
but the men have done this many times before
What are they doing? What are the rules?

Weaknesses magnified; escape routes blocked
tactics to ensure his suffering is mocked
pierced, humiliated and tormented to ensure
he's ready to meet 'El Matador'

A single bull, against all these cowards
each pushing their victim to the point of frenzy
encircled, provoked, tormented and stabbed
a premeditated act of Mediterranean cruelty

The inevitable stumbles, as he charges through the streets
a festival of evil, devoid of humanity
distractions provide routes for his tormentors to flee
ignoring this beast's amazing humility

His attempts to escape, confirm the futility
processes developed to frustrate and torture
a shameful spectacle of human brutality
a designed advantage for the 'brave' Matador

Starved and thirsty, drugged and beaten
En la Plaza de Toros, for the final Act
Spirit tormented, mentally broken
a sword at hand, ready to despatch

A once proud beast, now destroyed and abused
the appreciative audience who enjoyed, were amused
as eventually he falls, ending his ordeal
the roses rain down, signifying approval.

Natural Causes

Strengths and weaknesses, developed by evolution
balance maintained by natural regulation
nature provided food, water and climate
greed and ignorance now threaten to destroy it

Everything is superior and to something inferior
abilities and vulnerabilities, like Rock, Paper, Scissors
everything has its place, a purpose in nature's scheme
a natural Utopia, Nature's aspirational dream

There's a natural consequence for every occurrence
our activities risk an unnatural imbalance
a reaction for every action, or inaction
this the cost of human progression

Natural law doesn't allow for negotiation
there is no scope for interpretation
mankind cannot tame the extremes of our weather
when something is 'gone', then it's gone forever

Unintelligent interference by an intelligent bald ape
using unnatural means to maximise the rape
of the planet to secure profit from natural sources
pillaging the world and destroying resources

Such disregard for the animals, that share the Earth
what right have we, to destroy their place of birth?
Allowing a man to own and farm a field
to raise a herd of cows for the beef they will yield

Survival of the fittest doesn't really apply
if everything's getting ill, and likely to die
species disappear at an unprecedented rate
so many different threats to each creature's fate

Habitat stolen and devastated
natural occupants killed or evicted
at unsustainable rates, that will soon ensure
habitats and species are lost for evermore

Animals destroyed for a horn, tusk or pelt
as temperatures increase, the Polar ice caps melt
there's a reason why the water is not fit to drink
decades of ignorance have made the oceans stink

The sea is a rubbish tip, uninhabitable habitat
polluted, a poisonous and putrid vat
a home for the whales, the seas, the ocean
the origin of life is now a toxic prison

Articles and particles, abnormal PH balances
acid rain, buildings dissolve, unattributable consequences
so if nobody is individually held responsible or blamed
we'll carry on regardless, until our environment is flamed

There's a delicate balance, between hostile and habitable
everything has its place, its purpose and function
bacteria, bug, bird, reptile, mammal
but if one link breaks, the whole environment will weaken

Nature recovers from the natural events
extremes of heat or cold, are natural compliments
volcanos and hurricanes, natural creativity unimpaired
but we assault the world faster
than our damage can be repaired

But another risk looms, what if She fought back?
Or, has Nature already commenced her attack?
the waters rise, now our habitat is threatened
there are consequences
and on this Earth, we're imprisoned

The air we breathe contains so many ills
the water we drink, contains hormones from pills
the food we eat, is mechanically recovered
now all conspire, to avenge Nature's Mother

We've thrived and evolved to a point of domination
an unintended position with a natural solution
what next for Nature's 8 billion, ignorant guests?
A plague of all consuming, out of control pests.

Oceans

You wouldn't catch me
in the ocean or sea
where marine animals should thrive

Coz it's bloody filthy
with filth and blood
and I probably wouldn't survive

There's sewage and plastic
and oil and crud
and chemicals and effluent

Wouldn't it be fantastic
if mankind was not
so naturally destructive and ignorant.

The Climate Change Conference

October '21 we hosted CoP26
The UN Climate Change Conference
discussing issues that 25 previous conferences couldn't fix
in these 'Leader's', why should we have confidence?

The longer you wait, the more it needs fixing
the Earth's in a state, with sea levels rising
the land is flooding as the forests burn
whilst large corporations display little concern

A tiger's bones stripped and ready to crush
koalas on fire limping out of the Bush
cremated remains of kangaroos in the outback
natural balances that we may never get back

Record temperatures exceeded each year
as strange new viruses suddenly appear
with Covid 19 going truly viral
we're stuck in this destructive downward spiral

The icecaps defrosting and ever decreasing
the peat once composted, now burning, releasing
tonnes of carbon, and warming the planet
our time's running out, we're running the gauntlet

The air that we need but can barely breathe
the seas, don't risk going underneath
it's a soup of pollution, plastic and waste
a rancid solution, you'd wretch at the taste

Maybe Nature, awakened, is addressing the cause
is She culling the offender, against natural laws?
Climate catastrophes, flooding and fires
strong leadership, is what the Planet requires

Ignoring the cause, just addressing consequences
continuing to build bigger sea defences
as so many species struggle, their extinction guaranteed
we think we're exempt
committing suicide by greed.

The First Bumble Bee

The wheel keeps turning
winter frosts thawing
spring is awakening
the year is alive

Temperatures rising
nature reprising
insects are crawling
trying to survive

Nature, urging
daffodils emerging
each day is warming
providing cheer

(The) dawn chorus performing
blackbirds proclaiming
Nature celebrating
the first bee of the year

The Swans are courting
creatures, cavorting
nest building and mating
leaves on trees

Sunshine in the morning
frogs start spawning
nectar enticing
the birds and the bees

Bluebells ringing
the woods are now teeming
the canopy forming
providing shade

Dragonflies hovering
fox cubs playing
baby birds hatching
from the eggs that were laid

Summer arriving
lavender, thriving
tadpoles morphing
bats chasing flies

Bucks and Does
flowers in meadows
swallows returning
adorning the skies

Pollen dispersing
sufferers, sneezing
bees pollinating
nourishing hives

The haze in the morning
the earth, absorbing
hedgehogs foraging
midsummer arrives

The ants start flying
house martins gorging
sun rays, burning
clearing the haze

Caterpillars, crawling
butterflies, transforming
families enjoying
long lazy days

Lily pads floating
goldfinches, charming
bumble bees buzzing
cygnets on lakes

The Earth's axis tilting
the foliage wilting
Summer is waning
as Autumn awakes.

Hollins Brook

Today
the Brook runs in blue and gold
an oily discharge
from where untold
upwind in the Vale
an acrid smell
risk of death
to birds who dwell
within this stream
and on the banks
nearby where someone emptied tanks
and set their excess
oil to drain
mixed with gentle summer rain
encouraging the stream
'Faster, faster'
dispersing our own 'Exxon Valdez' disaster
via the Roch, the Irwell, the Mersey
sending the slick towards the sea
what chance for the Kingfisher
or the wildlife I see?
What chance for your kids?
Fish fingers for tea?

The Pen

She chose her cob
and they danced on the water
and He laid his claim
and they built a nest
and She laid her clutch
and She incubated
and He defended his territory
Whilst we waited

And He waited
and they incubated
and we waited

...and waited

And we looked at her eggs
and She looked at her eggs
and He looked
and we looked
and they looked
and we all looked again

And She mourned
and we mourned with her
and they were beautiful.

The Hollins Vale Swans

Seven weeks have passed
She's hardly moved
parental dedication proved
Her trance like incubation ends
their territory, He defends
the eggs have hatched
new life arrives
She's off the nest
there're 8 new lives
they've made it this far
now there's quite a crowd
this family of swans
the parents, so proud
with young to protect
and beaks to feed
the Vale is graced
we're lucky, indeed
the swans, that chose
this place to live
the community impact
so positive
The geese beware
and know your place
these swans preside
with effortless grace
I wish them well
and hope they prevail
The Swans that reside
in Hollins Vale.

Predated

Like others, I have waited years
to welcome cygnets to The Vale
the swans provided lockdown cheer
until last year's clutch of 8 failed

So throughout this spring, a nest with 9 eggs
brought mixed feelings to this community
the joy that comes when a new life begins
against the unease of mild anxiety

The eggs started hatching on the 4th June
and soon there were 8 cygnets present
such a contrast to the previous year
and a natural anti-depressant

On the 5th of June I made my way
to meet them and say "Hello"
with seeds and mealworm for them to eat
and to imagine how they'd grow

On the 6th of June, I visited twice
in the morning and then later
as all 8 cygnets followed their parents
for a parade around the water

So many posts on social media
confirmed how people felt
10 swans around the vale
caused many a heart to melt

But everything has its purpose
and Nature has no compassion
to allow continuance of all species
Nature has quotas and rations

So it was so sad and quite a shock
on Monday the 8th June
to see that we'd lost 5 cygnets overnight
to a predator in the gloom

A Mink, I think, may have been the culprit
for they stalk prey within the Vale
a callous predator, that shouldn't be here
but it needs to survive as well

Five little souls
over a weekend in June
lived out their entire lives

Who knows what will happen
to those who remain
the three cygnets that still survive

Life is so precious
like those cygnets we lost
because, when it's gone, then it's gone

But the one's we lost
will always be remembered
whenever I see these swans.

8th June 2021

The Coots

They mated
though nobody knew
and then they laid an egg
or two
That hatched unnoticed
then came the test
when they were led out
from their nest

Proudly presented to the folk
who tramp around the Vale
this family of Coots
such a timid bird
I hoped that you'd prevail

T'was such a lovely...
thing... to see
a family of four
but then...
just three

So both the parents doted on
their Punk Rock chick
their only one
but then he too vanished
where had he gone?
A meal for something?
Then there were none.

A Fork in the Path

Which way will you choose to go
at this point of division?
There are benefits with either choice
what will influence your decision?

A shorter path, certainty of route
your future, clearly defined?
Or to take a chance, that may bear fruit
what treasures might you find?

Make your choice and stick with it
be content with what you get
new opportunities will soon arrive
let there be no regret.

Fly Tipping

Shall I compare thee to a parasite?
A selfish lowlife, an ignorant man
Your own needs met, as you tip in the night
From a flat back truck or tatty old van
A remote location to mask the noise
Sneaking down a lane, or a public park
Mattresses, tyres, a load of old toys
Plasterboard and rubble, dumped in the dark
Garden waste, furniture, thrown from a bridge
They'll rot there forever, but you don't care
As you tip in the night, a broken fridge
Dumped in a river, a settee and chairs
A freezer; bin bags... full of dead chickens
A clear health risk, you don't give a Dickens.

Footsteps in the Snow

Only when it snows
do I fully appreciate
exactly how many people
walk through the Hollins Vale gate

Their footsteps recorded
in the snow
then frozen into ice
walking their dogs
recreation
or maybe exercise

The snow that fell
across the Vale
has changed the way it sounds
the deadened noises
flattened and dampened
across the hills and mounds

The Swans break through
the frozen water
to meet me for some food
the adults and their cygnets
the 2021 brood

The footsteps, evidence
if any were needed
that so many come to see
the Hollins Swans
I realise
it's not just the swans and me.

Into The Mist

Water particles fill the air
as fog descends across the Vale
a haunted land of dampened sounds
the colours stripped from dampened surrounds

A cloud, descended to steal the view
the route intended, now hidden from you
naked trees, appear sinister, haunted
branches seem like arms, contorted

Senses heightened through raised anxiety
a fear of that which cannot be seen
an increasing feeling of isolation
perception lost in condensation

You adopt the appearance of a spectre
your image fades to grey, then gone
as you walk into the veils of mist
now we're both alone, in this abyss.

Dancing With You

I'd love to dance with you
my defence, I have to plead
I really don't know what to do
and I'm supposed to lead

Because I don't know where to put my feet
and I'm embarrassed and self-conscious
although I think I have 'the beat'
I know I'll be atrocious

But I'm happy to be your student
if that's something you'd like to do
I'm sure there'll be improvement
if you could help me through

Show me where to put my feet
I'll do my best, you'll see
maybe, we could dance a waltz
if you will dance with me.

Legacy

I dedicate this poem
to my as yet unborn relations
descendants who I do not know
my future generations

If we met, then treasure those memories
of the times when we were together
and if we didn't, then I too am sad
that I never had the pleasure

I thought of you before your time
with a sense of love and affection
an unknown person in my family line
maybe a Granddaughter, or a Grandson

Family means everything to me
this isn't so profound
but I am always at my happiest
when I have you all around

The noise and laughter of siblings together
family times so loud
sharing your memories and continued successes
you make us both so proud

I hope my descendants, read these words
when I am long since gone
and sense the love I have for you all
through the verses of these songs

The poems in these pages
that give an insight to my life
and I hope the 'Me' you find in this book
is a 'Me' that you might have liked.

Spending a Penny

I went to the loo to have a wee
and when I finished what I'd been doing
I noticed some blood in the toilet pan
which hadn't been caused through poohing

I went to the toilet a few days later
the last experience still on my mind
and when I looked
there was blood again
not what I wanted to find

I got an appointment to see the Doctor
I explained to him what had occurred
he listened to everything I had to say
and then I was promptly referred

I went to the hospital on Sunday morning
booked in for a CT Scan
they concentrated upon my bladder
and the bits that make me a man

I got a phone call about the scan results
I discussed it with the Doctor
it seems they found something they're not happy with
and they want to go in through my todger

I went to the hospital for some tests
checked for Covid and MRSA
they told me I've got to self-isolate
they're admitting me on Thursday

I couldn't have any breakfast
not even a cup of tea
just a glass of water and a shower
that'll have to do me

I made my way to hospital
in fear from what was to come
the procedure itself, and what they might find
I wish they could go in through my bum

My Dad dropped me off at Reception
a day surgery appointment waiting
anticipation, anxiety
my blood pressure was now raging

I spoke to the surgeon, about what to expect
a cosy little chat
he did little to calm any worries or concerns
about my urinary tract

My obligation to my family
was really the only stance
that drove me through to have this done
otherwise, I'd have taken a chance

I was led through to a changing room
my procedure was right on track
I was handed some gowns, directed to change
with my arse hanging out of the back

Checks are made
"When did you last eat?"
"When did you last have a drink?"

"Any allergies?"
"Who's picking you up?"
There was very little time to think

A cannula fitted, an anaesthetist present
to set me off to sleep
some small talk
I don't know if I...

Gone

I started to wake, at first feeling fine
no pain, just rather tipsy
as morphine washed through my mind
I was told they'd taken a biopsy

'Spending a penny'? I'd pay a tenner not to
I'm frightened to have a pee
it stings and smarts, then bleeds when it starts
but I'm desperate to have a wee

I'm told it may take, up to four weeks
before the results come through
so, I'll carry on as normal, I suppose
I don't know what else to do...

A phone call from the surgeon, around a month later
confirms what I wanted to hear
the biopsy result was normal
there was nothing for me to fear

In hindsight
I'm glad I went through it
to get it off my mind
it was the right thing to do
to get it checked out
because now I know everything's fine.

(Whatever it is, get it checked, as soon as possible).

Man Flu

A man cut down
in the prime of his life
proves that this is no joke
but it prompts a frown
from an unsympathetic wife
as he coughs and starts to croak

Don't let anyone
try to tell you
that this is "just a cold"
the impact upon
the male is untrue
it's a horror to behold

This viral infection
discriminates
only attacking us men
there's no vaccination
to mitigate
this airborne pathogen

The speed with which
the fever comes
and attacks its victim's health
the Alpha Male
soon becomes
a shadow of himself

Crash on the couch
Wrap up in a duvet
and watching The Cartoon Network
The cure I can vouch
is chicken soup
nothing else will work

So see it through
for two or three days
is all that you can do
to survive and hopefully
recover from
the horrors of Man Flu.

The A&E Waiting Room

I instinctively look up
as I hear your voice
aggressive tones
the language, choice
whilst sat in the A&E waiting room
I cringe, as I realise
with a sense of doom
the chairs
there are spares, next to me
although I don't know you
and others are free
how did I know
you would sit next to me?

The smell of weed
and your attitude
your behaviour and angry mood
swearing with your child
sat on your knee
I know that soon
you will talk to me
swearing to God that you'll "*Go all out*"
bouncing your legs
why do you shout?

You can't stop talking
you can't sit still
why are you here?
you're clearly not ill
"ARRRRGH!... E'yar, did y'ear dat?"

your clicking shoulder used to start our chat
boring the room about the horses you chose
how can you sit there, picking your nose?

Why... do you seem to believe
that the rest of the room are so intrigued?
You don't notice the contempt
or worse, you ignore it
you seem to believe we appreciate your crude wit
and why on earth would you think I'm interested
in the fiver each way, that you have 'invested'
"9/2 odds, is that like 3/1?"
Our conversation will go on and on
The 330 at Kempton
you watch on your phone
you've backed 6 and 3
Number 3s nearly home
the final furlong, as number 8 comes in
'Unlucky mate'
but I'm glad you don't win

Your frustration directed to the child on your lap
impatience and aggression, poor little chap
your response to his continued neglected whinge
'Parental intervention', sees the whole room cringe

A young child, aged 5, sits nearby with her Dad
her life, so different to that of your lad
distracted, her apple, rolls onto the floor
she stares, intrigued
by your behaviour
the apple, recovered and wiped by her father
she just... sits there, watching you... fascinated.

494 Days

This story starts on the 7th April, 1964
a time when there was pressure
that Capital Punishment
would be used no more

On the face of it
the prosecution evidence stood the test
regarding the murder
of a Cumbrian chap
known locally as Jack West

Bachelor, John Alan West
lived at 28 Kings Drive in Seaton
A little village situated
nearby the town of Workington

On 7th April a car pulled up
outsides Jack's address
Police were called
the officer found him
battered and stabbed to death

A medallion and some note paper
the killers had left a clue
lead the police to a girl in Liverpool
the medallion's owner was someone she knew

The vehicle used was traced to a yard
confirming Police suspicions
that a person of interest they needed to trace
was a chap called Gwynne Owen Evans

Fingerprints found upon the car
linked Evans and another
a male called Peter Allen
both were known to each other

£10 cash had been withdrawn
in Liverpool, from Jack's account
Evans and Allen were linked to this
the evidence starting to mount

A gold watch engraved "J. A. West"
was found in Evan's pocket
when questioned he suggested
that he'd very recently bought it

The murder weapon discarded
after they'd taken Jack West's life
recovered on their route near Windermere
a blood-stained kitchen knife

Both were charged with murdering Jack
they stood trial before a Jury
on July 7th, by unanimous verdict
both men were found guilty

Mr. Justice Ashworth sentenced them
"to suffer death as prescribed by the law"
Appeals heard to save their necks
but the Court of Appeal found no flaw

In Strangeways Prison and Liverpool Jail
on August 13th '65
The hangman's noose tightened
for the very last time
as both men paid with their lives

Investigation, trial and conviction
it seemed an open and shut case
Justice administered
commission to execution
in 494 days.

"Dad..."

Every time,
you call me Dad
or Daddy
my heart skips

Every time
you turn your face
to kiss me
with your lips

Dad, come here
Dad, look at this
What's for tea Dad?
Dad, where's Mum?

Do you want one, Dad?
Can I have one, Dad?
Dad, where you going?
Can I come?

"Dad"
Such a powerful word
a title
I do my best

A Dad
a thing that I have become
an honour
I am truly blessed.

Rush Hour

Up at 630
not looking my best
showered and shaved
time to get dressed
730am
and I'm already stressing
I should have left by now
but my suit still needs pressing

745
Getting red in the face
I'll struggle today
to get a parking space
I get in the car
to start my commute
now stuck behind a bus
on its regular route

To get there on time
to avoid being late
got to be on the Motorway
by quarter to 8
so many different people
so busy and in a rush
pushing to the front
creating a crush
got to get to the office
and log on, on time
it's 820am
I've got to be there for nine

There're so many cars
so many empty seats
so many different tunes
so many different beats
bumper to bumper
causing congestion
queueing, stressing
pressure and tension
the 830 news
but traffic has slowed
I should be nearly there
not stuck on the slip road

The pressure increasing
to get through the junction
got to get through these lights
there's so much aggression
snarling and growling
risking and daring
stopping and starting
nobody caring
Satnav arrival time
905
that might be the case
if I'm still alive
but it was 904
another minute gone
I should be *on* the bypass
not needing one!

Edging forward
then the lights start to change
"WHO STOPS FOR A RED LIGHT?"
I scream in a rage
the lights turn to green
I manage to get through
and join the back of another queue
the road narrows to one lane
to get past a parked wagon
my dashboard reports
16 to the gallon

At last I arrive
as it starts to rain
my space couldn't be
any further away

Well over an hour
between departure and arrival
I get out of the car
and step in a puddle

The heavens open
as I cross to the door
my suit is looking
dishevelled once more

I walk in the office
late for a meeting
a colleague greets me
my reply:
"Good morning".

Wasps

The family sit around the garden table
the Barbecue lit, the weather beautiful
a sunny weekend in June

Burgers and sausages sizzle away
the beers are chilled, it's a fabulous day
an idyllic afternoon

A barbecued feast, now on the table
a family gathering, so delightful
until uninvited guests arrive

Wearing yellow and black and buzzing to be here
desperate it seems, to get into my beer
straight from a nearby hive

I'm sure they have a place in Nature's scheme
these bloody Wasps that always teem
whenever we dine alfresco

These angry little bastards with attitude
I wish they'd buzz off whilst we eat our food
and stop hovering around my tomato.

"Harry"

Always on call,
24/7
I see and hear for you
Dedicated,
since my adoption
it's what I'm trained to do

A companion dog
who gives assistance
and accessibility
We can go for a walk
and have a talk
despite disability

I indicate a stop or start
through the harness
that's on my back
My job, to see
and hear the dangers
that may come across your track

Always ready
constantly poised
to respond to your every need
A devoted friend
your word, my command
your safety guaranteed

You set our course
I navigate
to ensure your safe arrival
Dedicated to you
my training complete
I've earned my Guide Dog title.

Dedicated to my friend, Terry Finn, who volunteers to train puppies
to become Guide Dogs, including one called Harry.
What a wonderful thing to do.

www.GuideDogs.org.uk

Relax

Stop and think, for a minute or two,
about the things that are important to you?
as in, really... what really matters?

And see how many, are actually, irrelevant
do you need to worry, is it worth the torment?
they will leave your mind in tatters

Try to relax, have a rest
it isn't good to be so stressed
you need to look after yourself

So take time out and slow things down
take a breath, relax that frown
this tension is no good for your health.

I mean, I don't mean to be mean
If you know what I mean
But it would be really mean to mean to be mean
is what I really mean

My Eyebrows Are Going Grey

I'm blessed with a fine head of hair
and my colour has remained
My dark brown hair
some may say black,
has very little grey

But my eyebrows
well, they are struggling
and the grey ones
they seem stronger

They're winning a race
over the natural dark
and they grow faster
and much longer

And now I've also
got grey hair
growing out of my ears
I try my best
but they return so fast
I'm developing grey hair fears

I pluck them out
with tweezers, see
and now I'm back on top
but there's grey hairs growing
inside my nose
that I really need to crop

They tickle my nostrils when I breathe
you'd think I was picking my nose
but I'm really not
it's hairs, not snot
that I'm trying to depose.

Earworm

Half-awake and in my bed
an annoying song spins around my head
I need to get to sleep again
But to do so seems impossible
that I'll stay awake is probable
because of the chorus in my brain

I've since found out
and there's no doubt
the song only lasts for 3 minutes 39
But in the early morning
when I should be snoring
it seems to go on for all time

If I could only get to the end of this tune
a different song, I may then croon
one, that's maybe less catchy
But no, just when it felt as though I was winning
the needle jumps back to the beginning
like on a vinyl record that's scratchy

I lie in bed, my silent curses
this blasted song, its chorus and verses
repeating, it seems, for eternity
Not long now, before dawn starts to break
tortured in slumber and fully awake
and driven almost to insanity...
by this 4 hour, 12 inch remix I've created
of an Eighties chart hit that I hated
that's destined to last all night

I try to 'sing' a different song
but it just comes back, it's much too strong
I've got to win this fight

How did this song even chart?
and how did this earworm start?
I've not heard the song for ages
but it won't give up, it's on repeat
as I wrap my head up in the sheets
a battle with consciousness rages

This poem comes without disclaimers
just like that bloody song by The Proclaimers
but it may provoke some smiles
when later tonight, whilst you are sleeping,
your subconscious mind suddenly starts singing
"That I would walk 500 miles
And I would walk 500 more
Just to be the man who walked a thousand miles
To fall down at your door
Bah da la da
Bah da la da
Ba da da dan di da lan di da lan di da lar dar dar"

Images

The best image of me
that I can present
to the world, today

Is here,
this is it
I've done my best
does it matter what I weigh?

But you look at me
with that critical eye
no compliments to say

It doesn't matter
what I do
you never change the way

You make it clear
just what you think
you don't have to say a word

Any efforts
that I make
your opinions
are soon conferred

The way you feel
on seeing me
your face will soon betray

exactly what
you think about
the way I look today

So I turn around
to reflect upon
my reflection

And wish
the Man in the mirror
was a little bit thinner
and had a little more
self-affection.

In the Dark

Events in my past influenced
and diverted my journey
changed, I now find it difficult
to be the man I should have been

Events altered the base line position
that I depend on as my 'norm'
now I feel an underlying sadness
when I'm not quite on form

Despite everything
that I have
everything...
that I am genuinely
so grateful for...
once...
the 'Special'
wears thin,
I return
to this place
once more.

"With all you've achieved, your family,
everything, how can you despair?"
In much the same way
an asthmatic can't breathe
even though there's so much air

It's okay
not to be okay
So they say
Well, sometimes
I'm not quite right

So at such a time
I'll settle in my darkness
anything else
is just too 'bright'.

Mither

We're Madferit in Manchester
and if it i'nt a Faff
It'd be ace to sink a few Bevvy's
and some Scran around me Gaff

'Ave Fish on a Barm
or 'ave a chip butty
wash it down wiv fizzy Vimto
come round here for a bit
my Mam's gone out
she's probs gone down the Bingo

D'ya wan' a brew wiv yer tea?
Ey' yar, what yer avin'?
I'm proper parched, Aay, giz a sip
a jus wanna bit
am blummin' gaggin'
come on mate, get a grip

Mam, wos' for tea?
"Baby's head" agen?
Nar, not for me, I'm right
that suet pastry's hangin'
it'll do me guts all night

Deffo gonna 'ave a Ruby
their Madras is mint
it dead hot,
like
yer know woramean?
Can yer sub us
coz am skint?

Ave split me keks
I'll graft some Stone Island
I'm off fer a shufty in Town
Am brassic till Friday
I get cash in hand,
Nar, I'll jib on the Tram, mate, I'm sound

D'ya wanna piece o chuddy?
D'ya want owt from the shop?
I'm nipping out fer some Rizlas
jus' Sayin,
Don't have a strop

He's sellin' snide tabs agen
they look alright
but they're rank
she works there now,
that bint from the Co Op
I heard she's a bit of a skank

Hiya mate,
yeah, Safe
A've yer got yer birthday sorted?
Nar, I can't mek SatDay Bro
she'll go off her head
soz pal, I'm gutted

I'm gettin pure grief off me Misses
so I'll have to swerve tonight
buzzin for the weekend, Kid
but I'll have to skip, alright?

I was out last night
with a couple of bezzies
then it came on top with the Dibble
we had to split
so we got on our toes
and bailed out down a ginnel

Sliced about you and yer missues
but you have been tekin the piss
yer need to get it sorted, mate
she won't take any diss

Savage that she kicked yer'out
d'ya wanna crash at mine?
it'll have to be on the couch, you know?
nar, no probs mate, she'll be fine

Thing is, like
you know I don't mind
but at the mo, mate, it's just a bit hard
yer a top mate an all
yer know how it is mate
but she'll give us both a Red Card.

My Cat

A pussy cat
with 'Happy Paws'
this kitty is our pet
a kitten raised
he purrs so loud
and poses little threat

Then his claws protrude
from his 'Murder Mittens'
whilst sitting on my knee
There's a predator
inside his mind
and if he could
he would
kill me

Mice, birds
frogs and pigeons
are all his normal prey
but he'd stalk
catch
kill
and eat me
if he could have his way

This killer living in our home
who I love with all my heart
if given a chance
his teeth and claws
would rip us all apart.

Wordle #265

Five minutes to spare
I'll try this hurdle
Then hopefully share
That I got today's Wordle

Six chances to guess
The word of the day
Five boxes of stress
That stand in my way

My first try is CHEST
CH E & ST
CHT go yellow
E and S turn to grey

Straight in with a guess
As I opt for HATCH
ATCH are green
The first H, a mismatch

MATCH! There's another
I type out the word
The letter M is greyed out
As I'm feeling concerned

My fourth attempt PATCH
These words, they all rhyme
I press enter believing
That I've got it this time

As the P turns to grey
And my mood takes a dive
I could have had it in 2
Now it's looking like 5

My next guess is LATCH
And I press the word ENTER
A grey Letter L
Hits me right in my centre

This is my last chance
I only needed one letter
If I don't get it now
I'm a Wordle leper

I'm racking my brain
And feeling tense
I'm gonna try the Letter B
Let the typing commence

I spell out the word B A T C H
And submit my guess
The letter B turns to grey
I'm in Wordle distress

The only word I can think of
The word that might match
The only letter I didn't try
Was a C to spell Catch

Then Wordle informs me
The reason I botched
Was ignoring a W
That would have spelt WATCH

Distracted by rhyming
As my words were derived
The unpoetic injustice
Of Wordle #265

Smart Times

My memories of a time that passed
in little more than
a few decades
Progress? Maybe,
time will tell
what progress was really made.

Research for homework meant flicking through
the pages
of an encyclopaedia
When Franz Ferdinand
was not a band
and the playground was social media

We had a rented television
with three channels we could watch
we had it on hire from Radio Rentals
we all called it 'The Box'

We also had a telephone
on a table in the hall
it had a silver lock on it
so I couldn't make a call

I had a map, I'd sit and stare
at all the places
everywhere
and wonder
what it would be like
and if could I get there on my bike

Mum bought all our groceries
from the Spar...
on Sunny Bank Road
The shopkeeper would
deliver a box
in his van
to our abode

Dad might take the family out
for a drive on a sunny day
Mum navigating with an A to Zed
them arguing all the way

In the dining room was a radiogram
for playing albums and singles
on Sundays
Mum and Dad would dance
to their favourite tunes and jingles

Once, we rented a video camera
to film a special day
and after the event had happened
the film was never played

Every other week,
I'd borrow a book
from the local library
and read it on a rainy day
If there was nothing on the TV

We'd sometimes get the photos out
and we'd all become
'reflective'
Mum made sure
we didn't get any
fingerprints on the negatives

We'd get the bus to Town
to waste a day
if we were bored
and spend the day
just looking at things
that we could not afford

I'd buy a tabloid newspaper
and check out today's Page 3
I'd buy a birthday card
and Gary Numan's new LP

We had to have the right money
for any bus journeys that we made
or maybe just walk home
coz we'd
spent up in the arcade

I'd go to my mates
for a chat
and make plans to watch a movie
and so I didn't forget the details
I'd write
a reminder
in my diary

Something
that never happened
was a parcel getting delivered
If someone called
you confirmed
your telephone number
when you answered

I'd go to the bank
deposit a cheque
and pay a couple of debts
then nip in the Bookies,
check out the form,
and place a couple of bets

It's strange how quickly
things have changed
those times have all but gone
As it seems to be
that nowadays
we do everything
by mobile phone.

Smart Phone

Every place you've ever been
Every film or image you've seen
Every tune you ever sang
Every phone you ever rang

Every cause that you supported
Every relationship that was 'complicated'
Every drunken opinion posted
Videos of you intoxicated

Every drunken thing you've bought
Every idea your mind has thought
Every message you sent or received
Every fake news story you believed

Every Doctor's prescription request
Every appointment you made or missed
Every pound that you have spent
Every opinion you chose to vent

Every purchase review or Ebay feedback
Every internet parcel you tried to track
Every Amazon package that you sent back
Every person you know or work contact

Every word you say, it listens to
Every ad you see, it chooses for you
Every place you go, it surveils you
Every mile of your commute

Every 'thing' you bought online
Everything delivered with discretion
Every 'special' photo of you
That you protected with encryption

For someone to really know you
Then for things that should be known
They'd want access to your social media
And the contents of your phone

For in this device
is the real you
The person you've become
The thoughts and prayers
The likes and shares
It's all here in your phone.

The Barber's

There're all sorts of gents
who come in this shop
for a short back and sides
or a bit off the top

A 'Number One' all over
the clippers start buzzing
eyebrows are tidied
prestige male grooming

And a chat with the Barber
about what's on their mind
he's almost a Councillor
the two roles combined

The stories they tell
as they're sat in the Chair
Simon adds his thoughts
whilst trimming their hair

Football and politics
bowling and news
so many people
sharing their views

Births and marriages
divorces and deaths
redundancy and new jobs
getting things off their chest

He uses his mirror
to show me the back
but without my specs
I'm as blind as a bat

As I pay for my session
in the Barber's black chair
he's cleared my mind
and sorted my hair

I'm looking my best
and as I leave the shop
the next customer arrives
to get his hair cropped.

The Dentist

I have been to the dentist today, again
five times already this year
more injections to numb the pain
my lips, tongue, cheek and ear

I'd had a bit of trouble
then the agony began
an X-ray reveals the problem
the dentist showed me the scan

A molar on the lower left
a cracked tooth it seems, the cause
"We could pull it out or try to save it"
There wasn't time to pause

The old filling removed and lots of drilling
the nerves then ground away
for a triple root canal filling
my mouth felt bruised for days

But we're not finished there it seems
I tried to hide my frown
the dentist recommended that
we cap it with a crown

More injections, lots more drilling
then dental impressions taken
this tooth has seen me sit in this chair
for 7 hours, unless I'm mistaken

But on reflection, I have to say
my treatment was first class
my new friend, Matthew,
fixed my tooth
without need for Laughing Gas.

American

What is the point of a spell checker?
if the spell checker is, illiterate?
if the spell checker doesn't know how to spell
can it ever be legitimate?

Coz the one I use speaks 'English (US)'
is that even a thing?
Isn't it just English with
unnecessary Zee's in everything?

So I authorized the spell checker
and soon I realized
that unless I speak American
my words aren't recognized

Our lives would be so much duller
without Red, Green, Yellow and Blue
Imagine life without colour
imagine colour without a U

I have to question this behavior
and don't even start with 'Math'
because what you call the Trunk, is the Boot
and a bathroom should have a bath

My car, it runs on petrol
the central heating is powered by Gas
it's not a 'Hood', it's a bonnet
and your 'sidewalk' is called a path

After Summer, the season is Autumn,
you Americans call it Fall
and that game you refer to as 'football'
well really? It isn't, at all

Your bears and coyotes are big, it's true
whereas we have badgers and deer
but don't criticize our critter size
and your moose is a desert over here

You drive a route (as in shout)
in your Station waggon on the Highway
Whilst we plan our route (as in flute)
in an estate car on the motorway

You change the baby's diaper
You close the Drapes at night
You put rubbish in the Trash Can
And find your way with a Flashlight

But I'll continue to speak 'English (UK)'
to my American speaking neighbor
he wears his favorite sneakers
my trainers take my favour

It's just a bit of humor
but our humour doesn't travel well
no offense, but I'll keep the wriggly red lines
under the words that you think I can't spell.

Real Poetry

I'm usually lost
by the third
seemingly
irrelevant
and random word

Apparently
thrown together
without
any meaning
or structure

Of course
I recognise the true issue
Is my own
limited vocabulary

But I find
your superior lexicon
and your deployment
aloof
and exclusionary

I'm quickly left
wondering
what is meant?
By the crazy ramblings
of a mad man, intent

on delivering
an alleged poetic verse
presented as literature
or perhaps, inverse

Yet others
consume your poetry
and swoon, in wonder and awe
Whilst I
fail to recognise
any meaning
in your words
at all

I'm inevitably left
feeling illiterate...
that it's not you,
that it's me
because I don't understand
"real poems"
and your point
I fail to see

Maybe this is something that...
I'll get over
given time
but then another issue
I must confess
is a poem that doesn't rhyme.

A Frosty Morning

As the temperature drops
in the darkest hours
mist settles
on grasses and flowers
Then winter chills
craft new ornaments
a unique jewel
formed by the elements
Temporary decorations
born and adorn
the exposed tips
of leaves and lawns
Such beauty and symmetry
unnoticed so often
as the icy footpaths
demand my attention
Shattered panes of ice
crunching under foot
crystals of frost
coating the fields and woods

The rising Sun spreads its gaze
cold, to warm
dry, to wet
crisp, to soft
temperature defined separation
between ice and thaw
stones cast across the frozen lake
temporarily held
suspended above the water

in the 'death row' that is the tundra in shade
waiting to eventually
suddenly, inevitably fall
as if standing on the gallows
already condemned
fate assured
to be lost forever in the water below
upon the arrival of sunlight
by the hand of a solar clock executioner
a celestial second hand, ticking
sweeping across the land
as a natural sundial
marking time
with unrivalled precision
as white turns green
steam, briefly rises from a thawing branch
before disappearing, condensing
into tears lamenting defrosted formations
that drizzle the ground below
where a song thrush
forages snails
under the hedgerow
Unseen, unwitnessed, unmourned...
a stone, silently sinks to the bottom of a lake
relinquished by the frost
forever lost
as the sunshine burns across the sky
as the dawn chorus greets the start of the day
exposed points start to thaw
the crystal masterpieces melt away.

The News

A daily update, of misery and depression
delivered direct to my front room
interviews, accounts and interpretation
analysis and comment, with a big dose of doom

Local, national and international
on the hour, every hour, headlines reported
newspapers, Radio, Online and TV'
BONG! The Nation's mood is affected

Accounts and videos of what happened today
the spin supporting a corporate allegiance
sensational reports, delivered as rational
with little concern for any consequence

An Inbox full of disaster and turmoil
celebrity gossip, MPs indiscretions
hardship and suffering, Political upheaval
an outbreak of resistant, mutating infections

A 14-year-old stabbed at 330 am
"Over to our correspondent reporting live from the scene."
the story enhances the perceived mayhem
"Daniel, can you tell us what you have seen?"

"A close-knit community is in shock tonight
Additional police are patrolling the region
An anonymous witness describes hearing a fight
The suspect not named for legal reasons"

Plastic in the seas, *"To our Environment Editor"*
another High Street store goes... to the liquidator
MPs with Expenses, Duck houses, and Brexit
I don't know how much longer I'll be able to bear it

"And finally"..., the failed pregnancy of a Panda in a zoo
"And now for the headlines and the weather near you."

*"After the 2 days of sunshine, we've experienced this June
There's a storm from the West and it's arriving soon,"*
with a risk of severe flooding, so it's always a treat
to see a bloke sail a dingy down a residential street

And now, a Travel update in association with Esso.

Daffodils

Once the Snowdrops
have announced Winter's end
the bulbs resting beneath the moss
awaken, to send stems towards the skies
pushing through the frost

The Swifts and Swallows are yet to depart
their homes in sunnier climes
the daffodils already announce
the arrival of warmer times

An early reward for eager bees
nectar to nourish a hive
a reliable source, for a dependent bug
struggling to survive

As the sun casts rays, low and long
yellow flames ignite the lane
their trumpets blast amarillo song
to welcome Spring again

Spring pushes through, new life begins
the end of Winter chills
leaves on trees, baby birds
'A host of golden daffodils'

As the sun grows stronger and
takes a place, higher in the sky
the April showers force them down
the start of their demise

Bluebells, tulips and lavender thrives
Summer's floral display brings cheer
the daffodils recede, as May arrives
they will rest until next year

The daffodil, rebirth, optimism
as nature starts to sing
a Lenten Lilly, loved by my Mum
a joy, that returns each Spring.

(Love you Mum)

PAN(dem)IC

No milk, loo rolls or pasta
at Morrison's, Tesco or Asda
no hand wash or tinned tomatoes
at Aldi, Lidl or Waitrose
no eggs at the corner shop
or meat at the local Co Op
At the Spar, there's no paracetamol
no beans or chicken or mince
and when it comes to washing your hands
you've got to sanitise, not rinse
but there's no sanitiser or hand wash
and there's no football on the telly
the Euros are postponed until next year
and I'm starting to fancy a bevvy
But when it comes to the pub, we're all barred
Boris has grounded the Nation
this is starting to get quite hard
I think that we might need to ration
Because there's no common sense in this crisis
whilst I'm at work you've emptied the shelves
I just want to get food for my family
but you've taken care of yourselves
no one at Asda stops you buying
so much more than you actually need
five loaves and eight packs of chicken
how many do you have to feed?
It's getting like The Walking Dead
and now we're closing all the schools
people are buying extra fridge freezers
these are the real fools

Storing food, they bought but don't need
without regard for anybody
lives that are driven by greed
have no regrets for any bodies
I drove 35 miles, for a pint of milk
so my Mum and Dad can have a cup of tea
but I'm not allowed to visit them
it's video calls for me
their ages and existing conditions
mean they're holed up for 12 long weeks
I check in on them daily
and place virtual kisses on their cheeks
The Summer holiday's sure to be cancelled
the cinemas and restaurants are deserted
so many stores are closing down
and the staff are getting flirted
So I'm going for a long walk
I'll maybe feed the Swans
two beautiful birds, totally unaware
of the selfishness that's going on.

Strange Times

We looked to Boris
for what to do
most stayed at home
as they were told to
scared of each other
in the Supermarket queue
no doubt, this is a very strange time

Mother's Day cancelled
she's in Quarantine
exams cancelled
what will the Grades mean?
Will this strange situation
become our new routine?
The strangest, strangest of times

Football cancelled
video calling
holidays cancelled
hand sanitising
birthdays cancelled
clearly defining
these day as the strangest of times

The roads are quiet
and there's cleaner air
but the barber's is shut
have you seen my hair?
we're socially distanced
no hugs to share
in these strangest of times

At Morrison's and Asda
the only places I go
keeping a gap of 2 metres
as I follow the arrow
is almost impossible
the aisle is so narrow
strange, strange times

The 'R' below 1
now a national obsession
"Hello, are you OK?"
now a literal question
a mask that now covers
your facial expression
in these very strange times

So many have died
but there's nothing to see
the funeral of a friend
how can it be...
that I can't attend
with their family?
...
Strange times.

Thunder

Skies darkened
Pressure deepening
Clouds, blackened
Heavens opening
Thunderous crashes
Static tensions
Blinding flashes
Elec-xplosions
Bolts of lightning
Petrifying
Thunder bolts
Pet terrifying
One billion volts
Cum-nimbus lighting
Strikes and jolts
Senses, heightening
Torrential torrents
And static surging
Grounded currents
Ionising
In streaks and sheets
Electrifying
Drenching streets
Awe inspiring
Showcased for over
A Kilowatt-hour
A demonstration of the
Apocalyptic power
Of Nature... awakened.

Being

There is a thing
that I have
A thing... that is mine
A thing that only I know
or... I think I know it
at least, better than anyone else
though I don't fully know it
Nobody can see it, touch it or take it
it just is, what it is
I think I understand it now
I accept it now, as it is
and despite its flaws
it means no harm, to *any* other
for all its unintended secrets
the things hidden, so deeply, even from me
hidden, or yet to be discovered?
Will I ever know it all?
Character, preferences
the depth and complexity
the insecurities, the dependencies
the joys and the sadness
the regrets...
the darkness
the pride and the shame
confidence and emotions
values and loves
expressions and intuition
my reactions, fears
my spirit and soul
this, 'thing', is me.

Ghosts of My Past

Recollections of the things I did
places where I went
people who I hung out with
memories of the time we spent...

on pastimes, like Cubs and Scouts
school holidays, rides on bikes
street corners where we messed about
camping trips and Holcombe hikes

'Big' school, different ways
new friends, school days
a cross country run
a new stage starts as the last one ends
the team we played for, the trophies we won

A chance at 'The Offy' to get some cans
or 'chip in' for a flagon of cider
a ghetto blaster playing Telekon tunes
a football 'Twenty-a-sider'

The times that we were chased by the police
jumping fences onto Chaddy fields
managing to keep your dinner ticket
tomorrow, a free school meal

I think of you, some memories fade
any issues, long since forgotten
images of faces from past decades
people, who have long since moved on

First job, and with it, a chance to earn
many names I don't recall
new people and new rules to learn
I wonder what became of you all

There was a day, though none of us knew
when we were together for the last time
I can't remember when I last spoke to you
we are now all past our prime

Whenever I now pass through the places
where we met up and talked
I remember, your voices and faces
on the streets, where we once walked

Over the years, our lives have changed
shared interests, no longer important
we've all grown older, now middle aged
but our ghosts still walk the same pavements.

School Days

Some memories
of my school days
78 to 83
Does anyone else remember this?
Or is it only me?

A time when Unsworth Cricket Club
also had Tennis Courts
buying fishing tackle and air pellets
from a shop called Norlim Sports

When 'Alan Quine's' was a CoOp
and McDonald's was only in America
The Parr Lane CoOp was 'The Dragon'
and we didn't have an Asda

Escaping school at lunch time
to The Blue Dolphin for chips and gravy
the thrill of the fear of being caught
in hindsight, it was crazy

And Mr Berry's 'BoB Shop'
for Sandwiches and Pies
when everyone had a massive knot
in their Unsworth Comp' school ties

A Pastie from Mrs Reeves in her
Little White Shop on Hollins Lane
an hour sat in the Launderette
sheltering from the rain

Mr Softee's single cigarettes
smoking coz you're dead hard
cross country runs on a freezing day
the horror of the Knackers Yard

Teachers going to the Queen Anne for 'lunch'
a few pints with the Deputy Head
him having to nip out of class for a pee
it's no wonder we've got OfSted

Watching a movie at the cinema
The Classic, now a Halifax
The Odeon that used to be on The Rock
The Mayfair, is now just flats

When JD Sports was just a small shop in Bury
and pubs closed between 3pm and 7
there was only one restaurant in Whitefield
English cuisine courtesy of the Bell Waldron

Rebecca's Nightclub on a Tuesday 'night'
under where Tesco used to be
in The Millgate, it is now WH Smith
next door to HMV

Getting the 488 to Bury
to buy albums and singles from Vibes
a Clippercard to pay the cost
of your GM Buses ride
"These are the best days of your life"
is what I remember being told
suddenly, it's all a lifetime ago
and I'm 55 years old.

When I Was a Lad

Why was I such a dick as a kid?
Why was it always me?
The stupid things, that I did
why didn't I ever see?

Things I did, that others didn't
why was I so thick?
Doing things I knew I shouldn't
why was I such a prick?

Like running across the Motorway
three lanes at a time
hiding in a tunnel as a train came through
walking home on the railway line

It was me who hammered a nail
into my Dad's car tyre
it was me who set light to a box of tissues
turning the settee into a pyre

I walked on ice, across a frozen lake
because my Mum said I mustn't
base jumping off a garage roof
because someone said I wouldn't

Climbing up
to the top of the apex
between two houses... to see if I could
with my back against one house
my feet against the other
the risk, I understood

And it was me who practiced Golf
with real golf balls,
whilst facing the window
And I broke my arm
jumping off a swing
to see how far I could go

And guess who broke another arm
climbing up
on a three-legged table
and there are other things
that I can't mention
my occupation means I'm not able

Why was I so aggressive?
I had a real cob
I'd have a fight with anyone
why was I such a knob?

Why was I so reckless?
Happy to take a dare
irresponsibly
stupid and feckless
I didn't seem to care

In hindsight now, decades later
this poem sets me out as bad
but I wasn't you see
all these things and more
I did because I was a lad.

Mum and Dad

Michelle

H, J&A

X X
X
XXX

www.JeffersonPoetry.co.uk
richardeaston66@gmail.com
Facebook: Richard Easton
Insta: richard_easton_poetry
Twitter: @RichardEaston